Copyright © 2022 by Montez Johnson

Published in the United States by Winners Press, an imprint of Winners LLC, winnerspress.com.

Winners supports copyright. Thank you for buying an authorized edition of this book and for complying with copyright laws by not reproducing, scanning, or distributing any part of it in any form without permission except as allowed through the fair use provisions of U.S. copyright law. If you would like permission to use material from the book (other than for review purposes), please contact permissions@winnerspress.com.

The publisher does not have any control over and does not assume any responsibility for author or third-party websites or their content.

Epigraph and chapter title quotes attribution: Tupac Shakur

Unless otherwise noted Scriptures taken from the New King James Version®. Copyright © 1982 by Thomas Nelson. Used by permission. All rights reserved.

ISBN: 978-0-9712240-9-4

Printed in the United States of America

CONTENTS

Introduction	ix
1. This Is Not Mister Roger's Neighborhood	1
2. Dreams Die Quietly	11
3. Chicago Born, Mama Raised	21
4. The Fingerprint of Failure	29
5. Deadly Lessons	39
6. The Birth of Discipline	49
7. The Subtle Voice of Faith	61
8. The Road to Becoming Unconquerable	75
9. The Secret to Victory	89
10. Time and Chance	105
11. The View from the Clouds	121
12. See You at the Top	133
Notes	147
Acknowledgments	149
About the Author	151

There will come a time in your life – if you haven't gotten there already – when you cannot successfully climb another step without the help of a true mentor. A mentor is gifted with the ability to go beyond the curtains of time, see you in time, and then meet you where you are to teach you how to get to where they saw you in the future. This book is dedicated to my mentor, His Excellency Ambassador Uebert Angel. He is the reason why I can tell you with confidence that I'll see you at the top.

Never surrender; it's all about the faith you got. Don't ever stop; just push it 'til you hit the top, and if you drop, at least you know you gave your all to be true to you. That way you can never fail.

TUPAC

INTRODUCTION

You know nothing can stop me but loss of breath, and I'm still breathing, so it's still on.

I waited for just the right moment when I could ask him the question directly. I was one of five executives who was granted an opportunity to have lunch with the CEO. He was a college dropout turned owner of a nine-figure multimillion-dollar company, and now he was able to employ thousands of people to run and operate it. I looked around the table a little awestruck that I was sitting there. I had read about guys like Steve Jobs and Bill Gates who had done things of this magnitude, but this was an opportunity to sit with someone who had accomplished things that I had only dreamed of doing at that time.

I wasn't interested in the business-related conversations circling around the table, necessarily. I wasn't even all that interested in hearing about his company or how he overcame business challenges. I certainly did not expect him to be interested in hearing about what I had learned over the years. I had only one burning question in my mind. *How?* I wanted to understand the way he thought, the mindset that got him this far. So, while everyone else at the table was discussing business, I remained quiet trying to figure out the best way to pose a very personal question to a man who did not know me from Adam.

My heart began to palpitate in anticipation as I mustered the courage to change the direction of the entire conversation at the table. Finally, we made eye contact, and I asked my question. The chatter died down, and the eyes of the other executives darted between me and him as he began to answer. I was amazed by his response. In fact, I could write an entire book just trying to capture all he said. But if I could summarize everything in one word, it would be *character*. This, however, is not a book about character. It is the story of a crooked ladder with slippery rungs that I reluctantly climbed in my discovery of it.

WHY I WROTE THIS BOOK

The Cosby Show was not my reality growing up. Where I came from, that was for people who wanted to imagine being somewhere else or having a different life. But when imagination stumbled into the minds of the people in my old neighborhood, it got amnesia and could not find its way back out. The theme song of *Good Times* was closer to my life experience.

> *Good Times.*
> *Any time you meet a payment.*
> *Good Times.*
> *Any time you need a friend.*

INTRODUCTION

> *Good Times.*
> *Any time you're out from under.*
> *Not getting hassled, not getting hustled.*
> *Keepin' your head above water,*
> *Making a wave when you can.*
> *Temporary layoffs.*
> *Good Times.*
> *Easy credit rip offs.*
> *Good Times.*
> *Scratchin' and survivin'.*
> *Good Times.*
> *Hangin' in and jivin'***
> *Good Times.*
> *Ain't we lucky we got 'em?*
> *Good Times.*[1]

I identified with the struggles, but the 'good times' were an anomaly. For me, the odds of making it anywhere but prison or the grave were stacked against me before there was a me.

My part of town was ruled by the Angel of Fear. Most of my childhood friends were either murdered or doing time for criminal activity. I witnessed things that movies are made of, stuff that never makes it to the news. I wasn't one of those kids who grew up in the suburbs and tries to act like they're from the inner city because of the music they listen to. In my community, Tupac sung the lyrics of the lifestyle we were living. I should have been a failure, in prison, or six feet under.

I did not have a book like this when I was coming up. Even if I did, it wouldn't have done me any good. I wore glasses, and not the rose-colored kind that helps you to be optimistic about what you're seeing. Everything I looked at was through the lens of difficulty. My address was between a rock and a hard place, and

I just could not seem to find a way to get ahead, not even a little. But I had one main advantage: I managed to keep living. That left just enough of an opening in the dark clouds that hung over my life for me to eventually look up and see a small patch of blue.

This book was written to show you that it is possible for someone with my background and experiences to have a better life. I want you to read my story and say to yourself, *if that could happen for him, it could happen for me.* I want to replace the shades of struggle that you've been wearing and help you to see through different lenses; the right ones that allow you to view your life in the light of truth.

HOW THIS BOOK WILL BENEFIT YOU

One of my pet peeves is people who have made it and are selfish with their success. They get to the top and forget what it looked like when all they wanted was a break from the struggle and a way to get ahead. They only discuss their success with other successful people who already have the answers they need. They never share their process and mindset development that got them from down there to up here, or answer the crucial question that explains their present lifestyle of abundance: *How?*

I am telling you my *how*, but this is not a how-to book. It is a how-*you* book that tells the story of the possibilities of what *you* can become. It is the proof that even those who face impossible situations and circumstances can rise above the expected statistics. I am sharing with you proven strategies and life principles that were tried in the fire so that you can come out of your fire like pure gold.

Consider this book a B12 shot for your life to boost your core strength, relieve your fatigue, and give you what you need to thrive instead of just surviving. As you read my story, it will provoke a reaction in you to make a decision to go all the way no matter what the cost. Your eyes will be opened to see possibility in seemingly impossible situations.

One day, sooner than you think, you too will be seated at a table surrounded by people who are waiting to hear the story of how you managed to win big in life. You will sit there awestruck wondering *how did I get here?* Then you will remember this moment, because this is the moment where you not only turn the page of this book, but also a brand-new chapter in the book of your life.

ONE
THIS IS NOT MISTER ROGER'S NEIGHBORHOOD

The world moves fast, and it would rather pass by than to stop and see what makes you cry.

There were 818 homicides, 1,657 rapes, 22,171 robberies, and 12,514 aggravated assaults in my city the year I was born. And that was a good year. By the time I was sixteen, violent crimes peaked at 90,520, up 143% from the year before, and more than Los Angeles and New York combined. We were number one in the nation. For me, it was just another day in the neighborhood.

I grew up on the South Side of the slaughterhouse capital of the world in a neighborhood called The Back of the Yards. It got its name from the Union Stock Yards, nearly one square mile of a maze of pens, filled daily with cattle and hogs for the killing floor of the slaughterhouses. More meat was processed there than anywhere on the planet.

Over a hundred years of blood and guts from millions of slaughtered carcasses dumped into a nearby stretch of the

Chicago River turning it into a toxic sludge-filled waterway that earned the nickname "Bubbly Creek." In 1971, four years before I was born, the Stock Yards shut down, but the slaughtering continued. The killing floor spilled out into The Back of the Yards and surrounding neighborhoods. Gang colors replaced butchers' aprons. The "butchers" were killing each other, and the neighborhood became its own Bubbly Creek.

My neighborhood was crawling with gang activity, and we were bordered on every side by the turfs of opposite gangs. We called them the "opps." The South Side had a history of violence long before we got there, the kind of violence that forces confrontation whether you like it or not. Racially restrictive housing covenants and discriminatory zoning practices excluded Black people from certain neighborhoods. It was a fancy way of saying White people did not want Black people living where they lived. So they kept 80% of the city's real estate for themselves and forced Black residents into a hostile, parceled-out census tract on the South Side of the city that became known as the "Black Belt."

We got in where we could. My parents managed to scrape together enough to buy a two-flat. Two stories of terracotta-colored brick, a six-step stoop, an old wooden porch, and bay windows looking out on the street was the place we called home. My father let his cousin, Bluebird, rent upstairs because he didn't have anywhere else to go. We stayed downstairs. Inside the house, we had the safety of family. But the streets? The streets were another story.

The poverty around us was tangible. It was like blood in your mouth. It smelled evil. It gripped you like The Hawk at night in the middle of winter. You could see it in the stone-cold stare of the guy who would shoot you just as soon as look at you. And it screeched in your ears like nails on a chalkboard in the bitter words of those who could not imagine any other life but the one they were living.

Death was an escape for some, a place to get away. But for others, it was like a bounty hunter looking for the most wanted. And if you had the audacity to want to live, you learned to look over your shoulder every five minutes. Life takes on a whole different perspective when you believe the only places that would welcome you are prison, the grave, and Hell.

I never saw green manicured lawns as a kid. We had much more color on the South Side. On any given day, I could spot those little yellow plastic tents with numbers on it, the kind the police use to drop over the shell casings after a shooting. Red, orange, and yellow crime scene and police line barrier tape decorated my neighborhood, marking territories where gang colors clashed.

"POLICE LINE DO NOT CROSS." "CRIME SCENE KEEP OUT." We saw the police lines and the crime scenes. We lived the "do not cross" and "keep out." Gangs laid claim to turf that they didn't even really want. They just did not want any opps to have it. Lukewarm bodies covered in blood-soaked white sheets lying on a cold street happened so often, anything else seemed abnormal. It caught your attention for a few minutes, then it was back to business as usual. Police and ambulance sirens wailed like out of tune backup singers for the mourning women who just found out their son or daughter or man was never coming back home. My kind of town? Chicago. That was my reality.

Violence was my normal. I remember standing upstairs in the hallway with my cousin, just talking. Out of nowhere, I heard gunshots. It was so loud, like a giant whispering right in my ear.

PIYAH! PIYAH-PIYAH! We heard gunshots all the time, so we just stood there trying to gauge what kind of gun it was.

"That sounds like a .38."

"Nah, man. That's a .45 right there."

We were in the hallway for about half an hour before we realized what actually happened. We started hearing noise and sirens. We found out that there was a stick up in front of our house. A guy was sitting in his car, when, supposedly, some other guys tried to carjack him. He went to reach for his gun, and they shot him in the head, close range, with a big gun. They blew the guy's brains out right there in his car, right in front of our house while we were in the hallway.

That was the type of thing that happened all the time. It was so common, you just became numb, desensitized to it. You hated that it happened, but you were just glad it didn't happen to you. It was that kind of environment, that type of community. I didn't see anything in it, but I really did not know anything else. I did not know anybody else whose experience was any different than my own. It seemed like kids were getting shot every day. You got accustomed to it.

Anything could happen at any time, and you never knew if your next step might set off a gang-related landmine. A minor altercation could easily escalate, and the next thing you know, somebody is pulling out a gun. That bullet might not even be meant for you, but you could be targeted because of your association or proximity. You could be standing or walking next to someone who's got a bullseye on them and not know it. And the thing about a bullet is that it is equal opportunity. Once it leaves the barrel of that gun, it does not check your address, gang affiliation, gender, or age.

Sometimes people make it hard for you to do right, even at school. If you try to stay away from trouble and be by yourself, people pick on you. If you hang around your friends who are in gangs or into other stuff that you're not, people pick on you because, in their minds, you're guilty by association. You get labeled because you're hanging out with them. I came to the conclusion that this was just how life was. So even though I was still just a kid, I told myself you've got to be tough. You've got to be hard. You can't let anybody pick on you. I wasn't in a gang, but I felt like I had to develop the mentality of a gang member just to survive.

The Back of The Yards is one of the first gangster neighborhoods, so I knew all about gang wars. I grew up in a community where fighting was easy. You always fought; you had to be tough. That might have been why I was fascinated by action movies, and war movies, and the military in general. I think I identified because they so closely resembled what I saw when I stepped outside my door. Chicago was a segregated city. But it wasn't just Black versus White. It was good versus evil. It was gang versus gang. It was the takers versus the taken.

Every family in my neighborhood had at least one family member who was in a gang. Everybody I knew and hung around with was in a gang. For the most part, gang life was the default. Something as simple as crossing the street meant going in and out of gang turf. And the only thing the opps cared about was whether you were one of them. If you weren't with them, it didn't matter if you were part of a gang or not. As far as they were concerned, you were against them, which made you fair game. Nowhere was safe, especially school.

I went to a middle school which at the time was called John Hope Community Academy. It was just south of 55th and

Garfield Boulevard. The Boulevard was the dividing line for one of the rival gangs, and the school sat right on their turf. All the kids in my sixth-grade class were from my neighborhood, and they were all in gangs. We would all walk to school together because we thought chances were better for us if we were all together.

There were fights, but not many inside the school. High school was a different story; that was crazy. But in elementary and middle school, fights were outside. Gang members from my neighborhood would come at the end of school day and fight with the gangs that were in the school's neighborhood. That's just how it was. Fighting was a part of life, so it wasn't a big deal for me. But something happened that made me start to take it a lot more seriously.

I was twelve going on thirteen. I was heading home from school one day with some of the kids from my neighborhood, and we got to 55th and Garfield Boulevard. It was a wide street with lanes going east on one side and west on the other. In the middle of the lanes there was a grassy area with trees. We knew if we made it to the Boulevard, we were almost on safe territory. But there were times when the gangs on either side would fight right there in the middle of the boulevard. Sometimes they would shoot from one side to the other like a wild, Wild West shootout.

Some of the gang members from our neighborhood would usually come and meet us as we were leaving school just in case we got chased to the other side of the boulevard. There was a guy I kind of hung out with from my neighborhood. His name was Patrick. On one particular day, Patrick came with them. He was older than me, maybe sixteen or seventeen, about 5'9", slim with a big round head and big ears. At the time, he was just starting to get involved with gang activity, but what he did next was a total shock.

Patrick got a little in front of me, right next to me, and suddenly, he pulls out a gun and starts shooting in the crowd. I'm thinking, *Whoa! This is crazy!* Not because he was shooting at the opposite gang, but because there were innocent people in the crowd who weren't in gangs, kids my age and some younger, and some parents. Anybody could have been shot.

I was looking around in amazement just hoping no one would get shot. And for the first time I began to think, *is this it? This just can't be!* But this was it. It was the way of life. I didn't know anything else. I didn't see any other choice. I could either hang out with these guys, or I could be in the house by myself talking to nobody. That was it.

From that day, every time I remembered what happened, I thought, *Man, that's a little too far. I do not want to go that route. I don't want to be doing anything like that, not to innocent people.* But at the same time, if a guy came up in front of me and he's trying to jump me and I have a gun, I would shoot. At that time, I wouldn't have even thought twice about it.

I remember when one of my classmates got jumped. He came back to school the next day ready. He grabbed one side of his jacket and held it open for me to see, like Clark Kent revealing his secret identity. Sticking out from the inside pocket was the handle of a .38 revolver. His dad had given him a gun to bring to school. There wasn't a whole lot that was easy to get in my community, but guns were one of them. The .38 was popular, it had firepower, and as long as you could find someone greedy enough for a fist-full of dollars, these guns were not hard to find.

The look on his face said everything. *Yeah, I'm ready.*

I nodded my head in response. "Wow! This is really serious, here bwoy! Yeah, it's on now. Yep, we're good."

It was like that. That was the mood and the mindset of the neighborhood. At any given time, almost anywhere, you could become a homicide statistic at one end of the barrel of a gun or the other.

Death was hungry. There were plenty of close calls, some I knew about, some I didn't. There was one incident that I can say was one of my most "didn't know how close to death I came" moments. If there was a day that I would have been jumped, it would have been that particular day.

I had to go to summer school during elementary school. This incident happened to be on a day when none of my friends or anyone from the neighborhood gang came that day after school. I don't know where they were. Maybe they had a bad day or woke up late. Whatever the reason, they were not on that side of the Boulevard when I left school. But the opps were there, and I had to walk past them.

As I was walking by them, I did not feel afraid. I had this toughness about me. But looking back now, I know that was all God. So, I just walked right past them. They looked at me, and I just looked straight ahead, mean-mugging.

Just as I nearly cleared, one of the guys gestured with his hand.

"Ay! Ay! Ay! Come 'ere. Lemme holla at you."

I just kept walking.

There was a kid coming towards me from the other way. The spokesman for the opps saw this as an opportunity to get his attention and use him to try to intercept me.

"Ay! Call him, and tell him to come back." He motioned with a slight lift of his chin towards me.

"Ay, Montez. They callin' you!"

I kept walking. I was thinking, *I ain't going back there. I ain't stupid. I got nothing to talk to them about. I mean, they the opps! What I'm talking to them about?* And I just kept walking. It could only have been the hand of God that did not allow them to touch me.

It's one thing to have a close call. It's another thing to be told what nearly happened to you. That same little kid that called me out by name was a known murderer. He was known for sneaking up on people in alleys and killing them. Some time after that incident, I saw this kid going to the store, and he couldn't wait to narrate what *could* have happened.

"Hey, man. You— *Maaan!* They were about to *kill* you, man! Yeah, they wanted you to come back, but they were going to *kill* you!" He nodded vigorously to emphasize the point. "Yeah, yeah. They were going to *kill* you!"

The word rolled off his tongue as easy as breathing. I couldn't tell if he was relieved that they didn't kill me or disappointed. I just shrugged it off. That same kid was murdered not long after that.

I didn't think about death, to be honest. I really didn't think about it. I just lived. I was still kind of tough too, still hanging around with the guys from my neighborhood. In that kind of environment, something happens to your mind and your heart. They get lost, hardened, or broken; sometimes all three. As kids, crossing the threshold from childhood to young adulthood, we had to deal with puberty and PTSD. You're surrounded by so much violence and witness so many tragedies that you get numb. But you don't think about death until it hits close to home. At least that's how it was for me.

Things started to slowly shift in the way I saw my life. I think, subconsciously, that close call affected me more than I realized at the time. Something had started to set in. That was not the last of my close calls, not by a longshot. It was like, every time something else happened, a recurring thought was being forced from somewhere, a place I wasn't yet aware of or in touch with. But that thought kept coming until it penetrated my mind. *There's got to be something more than this. There's got to be something more than this.*

TWO
DREAMS DIE QUIETLY

The only thing that comes to a sleeping man is dreams.

There were eleven of us in my family by the time we moved into the neighborhood: Mama, my dad, who we called DD, and nine kids. Mama met my dad at the Bethlehem Healing Temple church located on the West Side of Chicago. They believed that as many children as God gave you was how many you were supposed to have. No contraceptives were allowed, so the kids kept coming.

I have thirteen brothers and sisters, eight of them older than me, and five younger – Mac Arthur, my father's namesake, Marvin, Maurice, the twins - Matthew and Mark, Marshall, Margaret, Matilda, Maxine, Melissa, Michael, and Marlon. With the exception of two of us, we were all born a year or two apart. The oldest is Antoinette. We call her Nette. She was like our second mom. She was the one my parents leaned on the most to help out around the house and to watch us when they went out or when Mama was delivering another baby. And then, of course, there was me, aka Bay Bay, number nine and the seventh boy.

Our house was bursting at the seams. How we managed to get fourteen kids into two of the three bedrooms is a testament to how we learned to make do. All the boys slept in one room, the girls in another. We couldn't do like they did on that old TV show, *The Waltons*. They used to take turns saying goodnight to each other. We would have been up half the night if we had tried that.

Big families were in my bloodline. My dad was the baby boy of eighteen children. His father walked out on them when he was around five years old leaving his mother to struggle trying to take care of her large family. My dad had always been tall for his age and muscular. So as soon as he was big enough, just before he got to the third grade, my grandmother pulled him out of school and sent him to work on a farm.

His childhood was sacrificed to calloused hands and the back-breaking hard labor of picking cotton sunup to sundown in the fields of Mississippi. Those cotton fields became his schoolhouse, and hard work was the schoolmaster that taught him the life lessons that became his legacy. He learned the hard way that when the man of the house walks out, the opportunities for a life with less struggle often walk out with him. Like the old saying goes, "The fathers ate the sour grapes, but the children got the sour taste."[1] He learned that if you don't work, you don't eat, so you better work hard. But the lesson that started his hard-knocks schooling was that education was a luxury for those who did not have mouths to feed. That was likely one of the most heartbreaking lessons he learned because he was forced to give up his education at a time when he desired it the most.

After that, my dad really didn't care too much about academics. Hard work beat out of him any hope for a chance at education. So, he could not read or write, but just like losing your sight or hearing, he found ways to make up for the education he never got. He was not book smart, but that did not mean he was not intelligent or street smart. He was both. If he didn't know anything else, he knew how to work, and he knew giving up was not an option. That forced him to become a problem solver.

When work dried up in the South, he migrated to Chicago with his older brothers in hopes of finding better job opportunities. He worked at the steel mill, but that eventually dried up too. He just kept on hustling and doing what he could to stay out of trouble, stay in church, and make a living.

He rented out a garage on the West Side and started working on cars. He was what they called an alley mechanic. As long as you didn't mind him running a repair shop without a license or any formal training, he didn't mind fixing your car. And cash only, if you please. If a car was brought in with a problem he had never seen before, he would figure out how to fix it through trial and error. There was no way he was going to let dollars walk out the door because he couldn't figure something out. He would do whatever it took to provide for his family. I saw my dad lay down in the snow to get up under a car in the frigid cold winter. Hard work was the creed he lived by. In his opinion, as long as you work, you're good.

DD couldn't read a résumé if you wrote one for him. He knew that if he wanted to change the path he was on, he could not use what he did not have as an excuse. He had to be resourceful to get what he wanted. He had to be his own résumé. So, when he found out they were hiring laborers for a big construction job for Comiskey Park, Home of the White Sox, that's exactly what he did.

The land was fenced off with a big fence. Instead of seeing that as a barrier, he saw it as an opportunity and made a small part of it his interviewing room. He found out who the man in charge was, and then he put a plan into motion. Every day, around 5 or 6AM, he would go to the construction site and "stand on the fence." With grease still fresh under his fingernails, he stuck his fingers through the fence openings and grabbed hold of what stood between him and what he was after. Hoisting himself up, he shouted towards the manager.

"You got any work for me?"

He refused to be discouraged by the raised eyebrows or allow the silence of being ignored to dampen his determination. He would stand there for about three hours, using every opportunity to make himself seen and heard, then go back to the repair shop to work for the rest of the day. Then he would get up the next morning and do it all over again.

That was his routine for at least two months. One chilly morning, he finally heard the words he had been hoping for.

"Hey you! Come on in here!"

His persistence paid off. He landed the construction job and became one of the best workers on site.

My dad might not have worked a nine-to-five and been home every evening to tell us stories and tuck us into bed, but he gave us something just as valuable: he did not leave his family. When a father abandons his family like my dad's father did, it's easy to grow up thinking that's just the way things go and follow suit. There's only one thing that can break the cycle, and that's a decision to do something different, sometimes something that is the exact opposite of what you have experienced.

DD never talked about it, but he must have made a decision to stick with us no matter how tough it got, because he never abandoned us. He usually worked six days a week, every day except Sunday, come home, eat, sleep, and get up the next morning to do it all over again. Sometimes he would leave early in the morning, and he wouldn't get back until late at night depending on how things went that day. Hard work had become embedded in his DNA. Maybe he figured if he worked hard enough, his children would not have to struggle as much as he did growing up. He did his best, but we still had our fair share of trouble, and times were anything but easy.

Growing up, we really did not have a lot. There were sixteen of us in our part of the two-flat, and we all shared one bathroom with a tub and no shower. If you didn't get up early enough to get in the bathroom first, you had to fill up a bucket of water at the kitchen sink and wash up in the bedroom. Name-brand clothes and shoes were out of the question. My parents did not have the money for that. My mom would go to the thrift store or to the used clothes store and buy clothes and shoes for us.

When you have six older brothers, hand-me-down clothes and shoes are the order of the day. On a good day, I might get something that was just for me. But most of the time, I would get the hand-me-downs of the hand-me-downs or the second-hand used clothes. That's just how it was, and we didn't have any choice but to deal with it. But the one time I wanted something new was December 25th. There was one Christmas in particular that I decided to take a leap of faith.

I was around six years old, not far from the age my dad was when he was pulled out of school. It was around that time of year when the push for Christmas shopping was in full swing. I would watch commercials about amazing, blazing Hot Wheels or Rock 'Em Sock 'Em robots and wish I could have toys like that. But it was like a dream that could never come true. Santa didn't come down the chimneys on the South Side. Maybe he was too scared he might get robbed or shot, or his sleigh would get jacked.

The only Christmas spirit I knew was the spirit of poverty. But it was Christmas time, and I got caught up in the hype. I did what most other kids do, watched Christmas movies and drooled over the toys in the well-placed commercials that they sprinkled in between the shows. After watching movie after movie, my six-year-old mind started to open to the possibility that maybe – just maybe – I could have something that seemed impossible for me to have. I started to dream, and I dreamed big! Even though I had no logical reason to believe otherwise, I decided I would try this Santa thing out. I thought, *Man! Maybe I should write Santa a letter or something, because all these movies keep telling me "Believe! Believe!"*

I did not know how to write a whole letter, so I did the next best thing. I got one of those glossy sales circulars that was full of colorful pictures advertising Christmas toys, and I cut out all the pictures of the ones I wanted. By the time I was finished, I had a stack of about fifteen pictures. That was my make-shift Christmas list. I wasn't sure how I was supposed to get these pictures to Santa. The best I could do was to put them in the mailbox and see if he would have the courage to show up.

Two-flats had one outside door, but when you got inside, there was a little vestibule with doors to each flat. The door to our part of the house was on the right. On the left, there was another door that led to the upstairs where cousin Bluebird stayed. Right in between the two doors was the old brown mailbox. My plan was to stuff my Christmas wishes into our mailbox for the carrier to pick up on his next rounds.

I peeked outside the door, leaned forward a little to make sure no one was around, then I made a beeline to the mailbox and quickly stuffed my Christmas list inside. I ran back into the house, heart pounding, and waited. Two or three hours passed, and I couldn't take it any longer. I had to find out if my list was on its way. I went back out to check, and there on the floor were my glossy dreams. *What happened? Maybe the mail carrier dropped them.* I decided I would try again the next day. The same thing happened the next day and the day after that. Each time my list would be lying there on the porch floor. The more frustrated I got, the more determined I was to see that list sent.

Now, in my house, my parents served double duty. They were mom and dad, but they were also legislator and police officer. Mama made the rules, and DD enforced them. Every now and then, they switched roles, and I was about to discover that I had broken one of DD's cardinal rules.

"Who put junk in the mailbox?"

DD was so mad I could see the steam rising off him. My dad was 6'2" and built like a linebacker. He could be like a big teddy bear when he wanted to be, but when he was angry, he could be ruthless, tough as nails. When he disciplined, he did not "spare the rod."[2] I guess you could say, a good whooping was DD's love language. If he did not see a mark on you when he was done, you might as well get ready for another round.

DD loomed in the doorway and eclipsed the room like a dark storm cloud. The "junk" to which he was referring was clutched tightly in his hand, and he shook it in the air punctuating his words.

"I said, who keeps puttin' this *junk* in the mailbox?"

This time, there was a little more air and volume behind his words. I was the one who broke the "no junk in the mailbox" rule. But I had seen what happened when he whooped my older brothers, and I did not want that to happen to me.

I was terrified. More than that, I felt ashamed, and I wasn't sure why. I stared at my crumpled wishes strangled in the hand of a man who knew what it was like to have his own dreams crushed at an early age. He called them junk, and I knew right then and there that I was not about to say a word. There was no way I was going to admit that I wanted something more, something better than anything I ever had or anything he had provided for me.

Looking back now, I realize DD probably knew who it was all along. Even though he could not read my name written on every single piece of paper, all he had to do was look at the kind of toys that were in the pictures and it would have been easy to figure out who wanted them. If he did know, for some reason, he chose not to single me out, but he made sure that I, and everyone else who was listening, understood exactly how he felt about wishes and dreams.

DD used to always say, "Nothing comes to a lazy man but a dream." In his world and in his house, wishes were for people who did not work, and dreams were destined to die quietly. The earlier you realized that, the longer you would have to get used to it. The only problem was my dreams did not die. They were gagged, but they were still there. My dreams and wishes were never delivered so there was no way for me to know if daring to "believe" worked, and that was causing chaos in my little six-year-old heart.

It's funny the things you remember. Who would have thought that a Christmas story gone wrong would wedge itself in my heart like that? It would take decades for me to realize that what causes dreams to die is the inability to express them. Seeds of disappointment and systems slowly suffocate your desires and try to convince you that you have no right to see them fulfilled. But just because you don't express a desire, that does not mean it's not there. Just because you don't talk about your dreams, does not mean you don't have any. But the fear of being misunderstood or looking like a fool can keep you quiet. Everybody needs two safe places in life. You need a safe place to bleed when you're hurting and a safe place to dream. Otherwise, both will fester and infect the rest of your life.

Christmas came and went that year, just another Friday at our house. But a tiny seed had been planted in my young mind. I did not know it then, but that simple act of writing my name on pieces of paper that carried the vision of what I desired set something in motion that was beyond me. Things had not worked out the way that I had hoped, but at least I had hoped.

When the Christmas season rolled around the following year, I looked at the commercials, but I did not dare violate the no junk in the box rule again. Nette had taken a job after she graduated from high school. She worked at Zayre, one of a chain of local discount department stores dubbed as "The Fabulous Department Stores." On Christmas Eve, she came walking in the door with a big black plastic bag full of gifts for me and my brothers and sisters. Mine was nicely wrapped in red and white Santa Claus wrapping paper. I fell asleep on the couch staring at the gift with my name on it.

Early the next morning, I woke up to my brother Marshall shouting.

"Bay Bay, wake up! It's Christmas now! You can open your present!"

He didn't have to tell me twice. I jumped up, took the gift from his hand, and ripped the wrapping paper off as fast as I could. There inside was a name-brand race car set, just like the one I had seen on TV. Someone other than my dad had seen my crumpled-up wish list.

I learned a lot from my dad, more than I realized when I was younger. I got my toughness from him. I believe I got my persistent nature from him too. When he stood on that fence refusing to quit until he got what he wanted, it was like an invisible mantle of that same dogged determination fell on me. I learned something else from him too. I learned that it takes more than a raised voice and crumpled up pieces of paper to kill a dream.

Don't be afraid to write down what you want no matter how far-fetched and out of reach it seems. Put your name on it. Look at the pictures that represent it. Even if you feel foolish, push past the mental boundaries that suggest it is impossible for you to have it. Take inventory of your thoughts. Imagination is God's way of showing you what's possible. Dare to believe even when it makes no sense. Dig your heels in and let your voice be heard through your fence, that thing that stands between you and what you want. Refuse to let your dreams die in silence.

THREE
CHICAGO BORN, MAMA RAISED

Even warriors put their spears down on Sundays.

It was around 3 AM, and I woke up to a familiar sound. There wasn't that much room in the cramped little nine-by-nine bedroom I shared with my eight brothers. So, as I got older, we would sleep anywhere it was more comfortable: on the floor, on the couch, wherever. On this particular night, I had fallen asleep on the couch in the dining room. We called it a dining room, but it was really one room with a space heater in the middle that served as a room divider. One side of the space heater was the living room, and on the other side was the dining room.

We managed to squeeze two couches in the living room, one on the back wall and one on the front wall, with a small love seat sandwiched on the wall between the two. We had a dining table on the other side of the space heater. You really couldn't fit much of anything else in there, but our family specialized in fitting a lot into small places. We pushed the dining room table as close to the wall as we could and wedged another couch in there. There was hardly enough room to walk. But there, in the narrow space between the couch and the table, was the spot Mama had transformed into her personal sanctuary, her prayer closet.

Privacy was a rare commodity in a house filled with sixteen people. So Mama would get up in the middle of the night and go to her spot so she wouldn't wake DD from well-earned sleep after a hard day's work. I could hear the sound of Mama's voice before I even opened my eyes. Her words rose and fell like a singsong hum that reminded me of the old church mothers at Bethlehem Healing Temple Church. She had different modes of prayer depending on the circumstances. At times she spoke barely above a whisper like she and God were swapping secrets. Sometimes only her lips moved as she shared her most private thoughts and requests.

I rolled off the couch and padded over to where Mama was on her knees praying, talking to an invisible God as if He were real. Her eyes were squinched shut, and the skin between her eyebrows was furrowed with intensity. If she knew I was there, she didn't let on. She just kept praying until her words gave way to a language that only she and God understood.

I got on my knees next to Mama and wrapped both of my arms around her left arm and rested my head on it. Her skin was slightly damp with perspiration, and I could smell the fresh lightly floral scent of Dove soap, her favorite. I closed my eyes and lost myself in the flow of her words. Listening to her prayers was the only hint she gave of what was troubling her heart. This was where she found her strength and comfort. This was where she fought her battles. The sound of her voice vibrated through her body, and her gentle rhythmic sway eventually lulled me back to sleep. I never knew when she got up and went back to her room. I would wake up the next morning, and she would be gone, leaving me still on my knees slumped over against the couch.

Mama was no stranger to prayer. She was what some would call a prayer warrior or an intercessor. She had a set time to pray every day. It's hard to say how long she prayed because most of us were asleep during her normal prayer time. It was not uncommon for her to attend an all-night prayer service at the church where she and a faithful few would shut in and pray from midnight to about five or six in the morning. She would take me with her most of the time, but less than an hour into the prayer service, I would be fast asleep until she shook me awake when it was time to leave.

She did not wear a prayer shawl. She didn't need one. She wore prayer like an invisible shield that she could raise up on behalf of her family at any time throughout the day. Every day before we left for school, she prayed for me and my brothers and sisters, calling each one by name. She would grab the bottle of anointing oil, stick her finger over the opening and tip it to get some oil on her index finger. Then, one by one, she would stand in front of each of us and smear some of the oil on each of our foreheads making the sign of the cross. Everybody got a fresh dip of oil. Then she would pray a simple prayer in a stern authoritative voice as though she was making sure any evil presence lurking outside the door heard her too.

"I rebuke demon and devil powers on every side! Father, I thank you for going with him and ahead of him and bringing him back home safely, in Jesus' name!"

For more serious matters, she would pray forcefully with an almost militant disposition. Most of the time, she would start in

English but end up in her heavenly language within a minute or two.

"Ha-tom mah-see uh-tah!"

She was like a commander giving missile launch instructions. Then, as if she could look with x-ray eyes into the supernatural realm, she would use her words like a sword to destroy any evil influences that threatened the lives of her children.

"I cut his head!"

Sometimes, depending on the severity of the situation, in her prayer time she would go into all-out warfare mode, battling in prayer for however long it took. She was not taking any prisoners, and surrendering was never an option. You knew she had struck a note of victory when she would open her eyes and nod slowly in affirmation.

"I feel a release. It's done now."

Mama was as sweet as an angel but fearless as a lioness when it came to her kids. She was bold enough to walk down the street in a gang infested neighborhood carrying a switch, extension cord, or belt in the middle of the night. But there was one occasion where I found out about a weapon she carried that was more powerful than a .38, .45, or any other weapon that was out there on the streets.

I remember the incident like it was yesterday. It was a late summer night, and I was sitting on a front porch, three doors down from my house. I was talking with one of my brothers and five friends from the neighborhood who were mostly gang members. We were laughing and talking about nothing in particular when, suddenly, we stopped mid-sentence, and our heads all whipped around at the same time. It sounded like a large crowd of people were shouting from a distance, and the noise was coming from the direction of my house.

I jumped up to lean over the porch railing to see what was going on. There was a bunch of people marching down the street with clubs in their hands. By now, my heart was thumping in my chest so hard I could feel it in my throat. We hopped off the porch and started moving towards the commotion. That's when one of the gang members we had been hanging out with on the porch recognized someone from a rival gang going into our house. *What is going on?*

We did not know what we were about to walk into. Meeting a rival gang member in the street was one thing, but what was he doing in our house? We found out later that one of my sisters had invited some of her friends to come to our house, including the rival gang member. Another gang member who we knew from our neighborhood found out about it and rounded up as many of his boys as he could find and headed to the house with sticks and bats and bricks in their hands. The tension was as thick as the humid summer air. These guys were out for blood.

The pounding in my chest had spread to my head, and my heart was racing. The worst possible outcomes began to sprint through my mind. These gang members were heartless. They didn't care whose blood they had to spill to get who they were after. Now they were outside my house demanding that my sister's friend come out or else they were going to go in and get him by any means necessary. My father was not at home, and there was my mother, inside the house, trying to protect a rival gang member – a young teenage boy – as if he were her own child.

My brother, who knew most of these gang members tried to mediate on the boy's behalf, but the opps weren't hearing it.

These guys did not make empty threats. They were about to bust inside my house and anybody who got in their way would be fair game. My brother didn't know what else to do, and we were both stuck somewhere between confused panic and angry fear. But inside the house, Mama was devising her own plan.

Prayer was mama's Plan A, and she did not have a Plan B. She did not hesitate to start praying as soon as she heard the noise outside, and she fully expected her God to hear, answer, and supernaturally intervene when she prayed. One thing about my mama, she knew how to talk to God when there was trouble, and she also knew how to listen. And when she got her marching orders, she moved into action.

She told the boy to call his mother and ask her to come and pick him up. She gave one final instruction before he hung up the phone.

"Tell your momma to stay in the car when she pulls up, and *leave the car running!*"

When the boy's mother arrived out front, with the car still in drive and the brake lights bright red, Mama walked out of our house in front of the boy. Her right hand gripped the boy's left hand as she half pulled him towards the car. But before Mama and the boy could reach the car, the crowd of gangsters – about fifty of them – swarmed on Mama and the boy like bees on honey. With the boy's hand still in her hand, Mama closed her eyes, and shouted.

"THE BLOOD OF JESUS!"

If I had not seen it with my own eyes, I would not have believed what happened next. Everything froze. The angry shouts became silent, and all the commotion came to a screeching halt. The gangsters were about two feet away from the car, some with their bats still in their hand but frozen in mid-air. It was as if a force was holding them in place. The boy got into the passenger's side of the car, and his mother floored the gas and sped off before he could even completely close the door.

I knew Mama believed in the power of prayer. I had heard stories about how Mama went to the store to get some milk, and on her way a man pulled her into an alley and put a knife to her throat. Mama had shouted the Blood of Jesus then like she just had with the angry mob, and the man with the knife let her go.

Mama was a veteran prayer warrior and she believed that the God she talked to every night would come through for her when she faced trouble. She was not afraid to call on the name of Jesus in the midst of chaos. And to my surprise, it worked!

What I had witnessed taking place with that mob of gangsters in front of my house was undeniably real and powerful. But Mama was always in church, so it was easy for her to believe. She wasn't exposed to what I was exposed to on the streets. So to me, her Christianity was just a religion. As far as I was concerned, if there was a God out there, I had never met Him. And if He was real, He was going to have to prove it.

FOUR
THE FINGERPRINT OF FAILURE

Everybody's at war with different things. I'm at war with my own heart sometimes.

I hated school with a passion. I hated anything that had to do with school. From as far back as I can remember, there was nothing there for me but a hard time. I was the butt of everybody's jokes. My hand-me-down clothes, the way I looked or smelled – everything about me was fair game.

One of my teachers even took time out of her curriculum to make fun of my nappy head. I couldn't explain to her that trips to the barbershop were never in my parents' budget, and the freebies occasionally offered by one of my neighbors were few and far between. And I'll admit, personal grooming was not at the top of my priority list at the time. Still, I did not expect to be the butt of a teacher's joke. I laughed, mainly because I did not know what else to do. But it stuck with me.

My school didn't have a playground; it had a battleground. And recess was where I learned firsthand what it felt like to be on the receiving end of words that were used as weapons. I was the object of bullies' attention. Forced out of group games, teased, whispered about, loneliness became my best friend. I was a loner, not because that's what I wanted to be, but because that was the only option left.

School, like the streets, was a place where rules were broken. If it wasn't the kids bullying me and telling me how bad I smelled, it was the teachers telling me how bad I was at everything they taught. In some ways, being at school was worse than being out in the streets. In the streets at least I was given the option of being part of a gang and being accepted in a culture where I could pick up a weapon and fight, or run so I could fight another day. But in school, there was nowhere to run, and the biggest war was the one that was raging on the inside of me.

It was the same old same old from elementary all the way through high school. The buildings were different, but the experience was always the same. I'd walk through the outer doors, crossing over from cracked concrete to asbestos tile floors, and head to the cell blocks they called classrooms. Each one for me was solitary confinement because I was not getting anything they were talking about. It was just hard for me to remember or comprehend anything.

I went to school because I was forced to be there. School attendance was a non-negotiable for Mama, and DD enforced it. Every school day I got dressed in clothes that, in my mind, weren't good enough. And I marched with the rest of the prisoners of war into a school where they told me I wasn't good enough. I passed first and second grade, but by third grade, I was literally failing every subject.

They told me that I needed to go to a different class for language arts. It was really like a one-on-one session. I remember walking into the little closet-like classroom like it was yesterday. And it's like I can still hear the dull screech of the steel tubular legs of the chair scraping across the floor as I dragged it out from under the solitary round table that was across from the teacher's desk. I would plunk myself down on the hard cold plastic and wait to hear what new thing was added to the list of stuff I did not know.

It wasn't until I got to the sixth grade that I found out what the class was. It was called a LD class, a holding cell for kids who were labeled as having "learning disabilities." Learning disabilities to me was another way of saying this kid is stupid. We don't know what's wrong with him, and we don't know what to do with him. So we'll stick him in here, out of sight and, for the most part, out of mind.

That was where my cycle of academic failure began. I was a LD student in third, fourth, and fifth grade. I failed fifth grade, was put back in LD class the second time around, and passed to sixth grade only to repeat the cycle all over again. It was a different school this time, but the results were the same. I was put in LD class in sixth grade, failed, and had to repeat that grade.

One time Mama came to the school for a parent-teacher conference, and I overheard what one of the teachers said to her in their one-on-one discussion.

"He, uh, he doesn't understand when words have the short sound and a long vowel sound."

That was the first time I was hearing that words have a long vowel or short vowel sound. I was thinking *This is stupid! How was I supposed to know that?* The letters looked the same to me. It was the same alphabet, so how would I know that the 'a' in 'bag or 'cake' were two different types of sounds? I had no comprehension when it came to stuff like that.

As far back as the first grade, my mind would always wander in class. The teacher would be talking, but I would be reenacting some movie I saw or something else. My imagination would just be running wild. If I wasn't imagining myself in a totally different place and time, I was preoccupied with the kids around me talking about me, or I was worried about when the bully of the day would launch their next attack. By the time I snapped out of it and tuned back in, I didn't have a clue what was going on or remember anything the teacher had said, so nothing was making sense to me. For the most part, I was just going with the flow. And there was this one incident that, to this day, I still can't figure out.

The layout of my normal non-LD classroom had desks in groups of four. So you would have two kids facing each other, and the teacher's desk was in the front of the room facing the class. On this particular day, the teacher called me up to the front of the class.

"Montez, what is this? What's going on?"

Our expressions were mirroring each other. She looked just as puzzled as I did. I was totally clueless. I did not know what she was talking about. Then she held out a paper.

"How did you –?"

Then as if she was too dumbfounded to continue, she pushed the paper towards me as if both she and it were demanding an explanation.

I looked at the paper like a defendant would look at the judge after he is handed a verdict. It was definitely my name on it, and I recognized that it was a test, but nothing else on there was familiar, especially the grades. I saw an A, and another part had a B. I was wondering, *what's going on here?* My mouth was partially open as I reviewed the page, but the most I could get out was, "I don't know." I had no explanation. I didn't even remember taking the test, to be honest. Passing it was nothing short of a miracle.

Well, my teacher took that test result as the signal of a turning point that should be celebrated, and she heralded my victory by calling my mom.

"Whatever it is he likes," she told Mama, "give it to him."

By the time I got home, mama's grin was as wide as the doorway.

"Yeah, your teacher told me about you."

The rest of what she said was muffled as she buried my head in the bosom of a big hug. But it was a short-lived triumph, like some kind of freak academic anomaly that deviated briefly from the series of failures I had already experienced and that were to come.

By fifth grade, things really began to go in the wrong direction for me. I was still getting picked on, but honestly, I just wanted to fit in. So I came up with my own little plan and put it into action. If I could not get them to like me, maybe I could get them to dislike somebody else a little more than they disliked me. I decided to become the class clown and make jokes about other kids who were getting bullied. I figured I could get them to laugh at someone else instead of laughing at me. But my victory was only partial. They did laugh at the kids I made fun of, but that did not stop them from picking on me.

By then, my older brothers were working. And even though they did not make a lot of money, they had enough to buy themselves some name-brand clothes, which I would wear every chance I got. But since we didn't have the luxury of washing clothes whenever we felt like it, sometimes I would put their clothes on right after they took them off, and I would go to school smelling pretty bad. That meant more torment. So since my class clown plan didn't work, I switched to plan B.

What do you do when you look in the mirror and you see nothing looking back at you? You fight. You lash out at anything and everything that makes you feel like you are a nobody, a nothing, going nowhere, even if the one you are fighting is yourself. So, that's what I did. I fought. I hid the pain of alienation and withering self-esteem under a mask of machismo and meanness. And in my heart, I resolved to never let anybody bully me anymore.

The kids at school still made fun of me and called me names – ugly, lizard man, anything they thought would hurt. But unlike before, I started calling them names back. I dared anybody to say anything about my smelly clothes, my hair, or anything else. I challenged them to touch me or try. I figured if I beat them up, the joking would stop, and it did. That left them with only two options: leave me alone, or get ready for a fight.

I had found a way to stand up for myself. I would use my fists, feet, or whatever else I could get my hands on, to prove to them that I was a one-man army and not someone to mess with. I was done letting them get away with making fun of me. I'd give them one "Step off me!" warning, and if they did not listen, I'd take that as an invitation to fight. And fighting was one subject I did not plan to fail.

I had more than a few takers which made me a familiar face in the principal's office and started a string of fight-related school suspensions, more than I care to remember. And by the time I reached the seventh grade, I was labeled a "bad kid" who could barely read and write. The only thing I was passing in was failure, and I carried that report card into the next grade.

Imagine going to school and you're in the same class with your sister who is supposed to be two years behind you. You sit in the classes day in and day out, but you still don't comprehend anything. Then you dodge your way through opps turf to get back home only to hang out with friends who were doing stuff you knew deep down inside you had no business doing. But everybody else was doing it, and I did not want to be the odd man out in school *and* at home.

My self-esteem was suffocating, and I saw very little value in myself. There was just so much going on, and trouble was finding me everywhere I went. Kids my age – some of them friends of mine – were getting murdered or facing life sentences. I did not want to do stuff that got me locked in a cell or a coffin. At the same time, the streets were like an obsessive, insecure lover that thinks you might try to break off the relationship. The streets had me on speed dial. I knew I could probably be the best gang member in the community if I wanted to. The problem was, I did not want to, but I did not know what else to do.

It was a battle, an internal struggle, and I started to feel like my life was over before it really got started. I was still practically a kid, but inside I felt like an old man that life had beat down over the years. As far as I could tell, my options were limited to slim and none. To be honest, I was done with life. But then something unexpected happened through a message that wasn't even meant for me.

Of all the places to have a life-changing moment, I never expected a closet to be one of them. I walked into the nine-by-nine bedroom that I shared with my eight brothers and went over to the narrow closet. We did not know anything about walk-in closets back then. It was more like a lean-in or reach-in closet. I was looking for a mate to a shoe, and since there was no light in the closet, I opened the makeshift curtains wider so I could let more light in from the window.

The closet was so small, all my brothers' stuff was piled up in there because we did not clean our room. As you can imagine, there were a lot of shoes to dig through. So I got down on the floor and started to work my way through the pile. While I was on my knees, I was just thinking about my life. *I'm tired of living like this. All my clothes are my brothers'. Man, this is crazy! This ain't life!* By now I'm flinging shoes out of the way. The more I contemplated my personal life, school life, and street life, the more frustrated and desperate I felt. *Mama, she don't even know the life I'm living. She's in church so much, she can't even see straight. She's not exposed to what I'm exposed to. She has no clue what I'm going through. And even if I tried to tell her, she won't understand m—.*

It was like someone pressed pause on my mental tirade. Just as I was about to reach for another shoe, the light from the window drew my eyes to something unfamiliar in the heap of various sized shoes. I leaned a little further into the closet to pick it up. It was a piece of wrinkled up notebook paper. As I drew it closer to my face, even though I could barely read, I recognized my mother's handwriting.

THE FINGERPRINT OF FAILURE

It was a letter written in cursive. I don't know how it got into our closet, but it must have been there a while or been written a while back because the pencil was faded. The once dark charcoal graphite was now a washed-out gray. I was already partially inside the closet, so I found a spot that had a little less clutter and sat with my back leaned against the side wall.

I remembered that Mama would sometimes write out her prayers to God as I strained to make out the words on the page.

"God, you know what I been through, and how You are there to keep us."

That was about all I could make out. I sat there staring at the page half confused, half marveling that Mama believed God was real enough for her to write a note to Him. *Did she actually believe He would read it?*

There was no way I could write a letter to God on my own. But I was desperate enough to try something different. I really wanted to know if there was a God or if what my mother believed was just a religion, so to speak. I knew Mama believed in God, but I could not see any tangible evidence of His existence given my circumstances at the time. For the first time, I wanted to give this God a chance to prove Himself. I didn't know the proper protocol in addressing Him, so I just started talking.

"God, if You're real, please help me."

And then I waited.

I did not hear the blast of an angelic messenger's trumpet. I did not hear thunder or see a bright light. God did not come down from the clouds or anything like that. It was just silent, like every sound on Earth was hushed, and my words had been swallowed up in nothingness. My mouth closed, but my mind was still reaching out in desperation. *Lord, if You are real, I should not have to tell anybody. I should not have to go to church. But I promise You, if You are real, come into my life. If you are real, do something in my life.* And that's when the tears began to flow.

I felt vulnerable and gullible, like I had fallen for some kind of celestial scam. *This is just a waste of time! If He is real and not just some good idea, He should be able to hear me sitting here on the floor in this small bedroom closet with tears streaming down my face.* I could not stop the tears. I don't even know why I was crying. I sat there in that closet for a little longer, minutes that felt like forever, and I waited for God to show up. I really waited for Him to show up. But nothing happened. Well, at least that's what I thought.

It is said that coincidence is when God chooses to remain anonymous. Was it a coincidence that I found my mother's handwritten note on the closet floor buried under a heap of mismatched shoes? Was it coincidence that the only words I could make out on the page echoed the deepest sentiment of my heart? "God you know what I been through …" I can't say for sure. But one thing is certain, little by little, things began to change.

FIVE
DEADLY LESSONS

If God wanted me to be quiet He would've never showed me what He does.

In Chicago, it starts to get cool in the Fall. That's nothing out of the ordinary, but this Friday morning seemed to have a little extra bite to the chilly air. It was the 20th of November, '92. I got up and got ready just as I would any other school day and made the fourteen-minute walk to South Union Avenue.

Tilden High was an imposing structure, three-and-a-half stories of limestone and red brick, pilasters topped by Ionic capitals, and arch-topped windows. But once inside the prominent cornice-crowned entrance and pedimented parapet walls, you were greeted with randomly operative metal detectors that were your first clue that school was a potential death trap.

Tilden was no stranger to violence. It had a history checkered with racial tension, student demonstrations, and all-out brawls both inside and outside the school walls. I saw a lot of fights in this school. Too many. I've seen five guys jumping on one guy. Sometimes there would be five, six, eight, maybe ten students brawling at the same time. There were multiple gangs represented in this school, but there was one predominant gang from the area I grew up, and that was the Black P. Stones. When you had P. Stones, Mickey Cobras and Vice Lords walking the same halls, you knew it was only a matter of time before the next war broke out.

School was a breeding ground for gang warfare, so it was not uncommon to see blood shed on those checkerboard floors. By the time a kid got to high school, his gang affiliation became his identity, and a few words exchanged between opps could turn into an all-out gang war. With gang wars, it's blood for blood. If one gang member takes a hit, the shooters in the gang take action. So it was a constant back and forth: someone gets killed, and the members of the gang go back the same day or the next day to retaliate. Back and forth, back and forth, that's how it was.

The atmosphere was always tense because you knew anything was liable to happen at any time. If there were ten boys in a classroom, seven of them would be gang members, minimum. In some cases, eight, nine, or all ten of them would be gang members. So roughly seventy to eighty percent of the students were involved with a gang. Fights were a daily thing; I saw them all the time. But on that chilly morning, it was what I heard that caught my attention.

Typically, you had about five minutes in between classes to get from one class to the other. Most of the time, I did not need anything from my locker, but I would stop there anyway, chitchatting or just hanging around until it was time to go to my next class. As I was standing there at my locker, a sound rang through the air. *KAK! KAK-KAK!* My first thought was *who in the world could be bringing fireworks to school?* I knew what gunshots sounded like when you're outside, but what I heard wasn't quite the same. Then I heard girls screaming and the sound of kids running.

Not far from my locker was a shortcut to the other side of the building. That's where it seemed all the noise was coming from. I was on the third floor, but the commotion was on the second floor, so I went down to get a closer look. It was pandemonium! Kids were running everywhere, some of them were running towards me to get away from whatever had happened. *What's going on here? Fireworks can't be that bad.* And so I continued walking towards the direction everybody else was running away from. By the time I got near to the scene of the incident, I could hear kids reporting.

"Oh! No!"

"No no no no no!"

"Oooh! Oooh! Oooh!"

It was clear that this was more than a mischievous fireworks prank. Other kids were starting to come out of the classrooms to join the onlookers. I pushed my way through the crowd so I could see for myself what was going on. And there on the ground were two boys still wearing their Fall jackets. One of them I recognized.

The taller kid looked like he could have been a sophomore, possibly a junior. He was lying on his side with his knees drawn up in a fetal-like position. His eyes were still open, and I could see nothing but fear in them. The other kid was kind of short and a little heavyset. He was a freshman. I never met him personally, but I would see him every now and again around the neighborhood. Now he was lying flat on his stomach in a pool of blood. His pants were wet, and there was a puddle of urine mixing with the blood spots on the floor next to him. He had been shot in the back. I stood there thinking about the times I had seen him around school. It was barely 10AM, but the eyes of DeLondyn Lawson were closed for good.

One of the teachers came out of his classroom.

"Hey, what's going on? What's going on? Can you get to your class?"

Nobody was moving. He cleared a path through the crowd of students, some crying, some shaking their heads.

"Hey! What's going on here? Wha — Whoa!"

The scene in front of him gave him all the explanation he needed.

"No, no! Get out! Everybody, get out! Get up and move! Move! Go back to your class!"

He dropped down next to where the boys were lying, and he began to feel each kid's neck to see if he could get a pulse. There was so much commotion still going on, kids moving away, others trying to get a closer look. That's when the hall monitors showed up and started rallying the kids to go to their division classes.

Principal Steward's voice over the loudspeaker pierced through the chaos.

"At this time, we're going to ask that students and staff proceed to conduct an internal lockdown. This is not a drill! I repeat, this is not a drill! 9-1-1 has been called. Remain in internal lockdown until instructed otherwise by a uniformed officer."

I made my way to my division class down on the first floor to wait out the lockdown. The classroom was buzzing about what had happened. I was just sitting there wondering why that had happened and hoping the other kid survived. It was a sad story, but one with which I was too familiar. Seeing people die was commonplace for me.

As volatile as the school environment was known to be, there were no police officers onsite to man the metal detectors, so they were usually turned off. Maybe that's what the shooter was counting on. After the incident, the freshman was found hiding under the porch of a house across the street from the school. He was later tried as an adult and sentenced to forty-five years. They had the metal detectors on every day after that.

The bullet that struck DeLondyn in the back pierced his heart and ended the life of the fifteen-year-old freshman almost instantly. He was an innocent bystander, later described as a boy who was trying to stay away from gangs. He was probably walking away from the gang-related argument between the sixteen-year-old freshman shooter and some other gang members when he was shot in the back.

Before his death, Delondyn had been attending funerals for boys he knew at a rate of one or two a month. Like me, he wasn't in a gang, but his friends were, and every month, somebody he knew in his age group was dying. Some of the news reports said DeLondyn was "in the wrong place at the wrong time," which made me wonder, if school is the wrong place, where is the *right* place?

We lived in a community where you never knew who was going to make it back to school the next day because there were so many drive-by shootings. Some would survive, some wouldn't. If they were determined enough, some gang members would stake out the house of the person they were after and hide in the gangways. Then as soon as the person came out of the house, *Boom! Boom! Boom!* It's over.

Most of my classmates didn't make it to graduation. It's not that they did not get the grades. They did not live long enough. My freshman class was over five hundred students. But by the time we got to our senior year, there were barely a hundred and twenty of us. Of all the friends from around the block that I hung out with in elementary school, I am the only one that graduated from high school; the only one.

I didn't put two and two together until much later, but ever since my closet encounter, things had started changing. My desire to escape the street life began to get stronger. It was like I was becoming a different person, and there was no one else like me. I felt like I was in an alien nation, and I had a one-track mind to go somewhere and do something better. I just did not know what it was. I told myself I'll know it when I see it.

I started doing strange things. Not that I wanted to; I just found myself doing them. I remember picking up a Bible and trying to read it. One thing that had not changed in my closet encounter was my reading skills. Even though I picked up the Bible, I did not know what I was reading, or, I should say, *trying* to read. Half the words I couldn't make out, but for some strange reason, I just kept trying. I did not understand a word of it, but something was drawing me to it. I attempted to share with some of the guys what was happening, but they laughed me to scorn. There was nothing cool about reading the Bible. But these spontaneous thoughts – I call them impressions – just kept coming.

There was like an invisible tug of war going on, something pulling me away from the life I knew. Something inside was nudging me, *No, don't go there. No, no. Don't do that.* It got to the point where I did not want to hang out with my old friends anymore. We called ourselves friends, but there was always an element of distrust. We all knew it. That was just life.

These impressions were like a safety at an intersection trying to get me to cross the busy street of life as I knew it to some unknown territory. They seemed to caution me to stay out of trouble, which meant staying away from the guys I knew. Once again, I was being called into alienation, and found myself making decisions that created an even wider divide between the me I was and who I was becoming.

I did not understand this strange new alter ego. He did not make sense to me. But I didn't know it was going to mess with my "love" life too. I considered myself a normal teenager. The only thing outrunning my raging hormones was my desire to escape the street life. But I never expected that a girl would be the one to prove just how desperate I was.

Most guys pick a girl they want to get with. I picked a girl to get away from the guys in the neighborhood. Her name was Beonce. To say she came from a broken family is an understatement, but that was the status quo. Her mom was not married but preferred married men, and she did not let that get in the way of having three girls with three different fathers. That's what people did where I came from, so it wasn't a big deal to me at the time. Her mom was kind of strict, meaning if she left the house, I had to leave the house. But on this particular day, she made an exception. What happened next proved beyond any shadow of doubt just how much change had taken place.

It was a small two-bedroom apartment. Beonce's mom had one of the bedrooms, and the girls slept in the other. Her mom had to go out to meet her boyfriend, so she left us under the supervision of her thirty-something, openly gay cousin we called "Uncle." Let's just say Uncle had a very liberal attitude towards sex.

Beonce shared a bedroom with her two younger sisters, and we were all in the girls' room watching TV when Uncle came in. He looked in the direction of the two younger sisters.

"Y'all come out."

His androgynous tone dragged our eyes away from the TV.

"Let them alone, and let them enjoy themselves."

With that, he ushered the younger girls out of the room and closed the door leaving me and Beonce to do what he expected us to do.

I did not need any additional encouragement, and she seemed willing, so I went for it. But something deep inside began to bother me. I couldn't quite put my finger on it, and I couldn't shake it. I tried, I mean I *really* tried, but I couldn't. As bad as my nature wanted to do what for me was the natural thing to do, I couldn't go through with it. Instead, I started having a conversation with her.

It honestly felt like I was having an out of body experience, because I'm thinking, *what are you doing, man?* But my mouth seemed to have taken on a life of its own. Words were just coming out without checking with me to see if I was okay with it or if they made any sense, and I'm thinking *where did that come from?* So, instead of doing what most teenage boys dream of doing, we just sat there chatting. Worse yet, I ended up lecturing her.

"Has your mother ever talked to you about, you know, sex?"

"No." She sat quietly, not knowing what was going to happen next.

"Well, let me give you some advice."

Inside, this was starting to freak me out. It was like my mouth was on autopilot, and the words kept coming.

"Well, I don't think you should do it until you're married."

We were both stunned. *Jesus Christ! That had to be the stupidest thing I could have ever said!* What was even more strange is that deep down inside, I knew I meant every word, though I didn't understand why.

What happened that day with Beonce convinced me once and for all that something had happened in that closet for sure. I don't know what would have happened if Beonce and I had done what I wanted to do that day, but I found out later that her name means *a trap*. Maybe I would have helped to perpetuate her mother's cycle and ended up a teen-aged father like so many of the guys I knew.

Change often requires your consent, but not always your permission. I had asked God to do something in my life, and He was doing it whether I liked it or not. None of it was making sense. Picking up a Bible I couldn't read. Walking away from a girl that was practically handed to me on a platter. That nagging feeling of wanting something better but not knowing what it was. And those impressions that marked the beginning of the end of life as I knew it.

I was moving tentatively not knowing what to expect next. It was like starting somewhere in the middle of a war zone and making the necessary adjustments as you go. I needed a plan. I did not want to end up like DeLondyn. Seeing what happened to him taught me that sometimes just trying to walk away from trouble can get you in trouble. So, I decided to try running. But first, I needed a new identity.

SIX
THE BIRTH OF DISCIPLINE

Happy are those who dream dreams and are ready to pay the price to make them come true.

"You have to know how to hit, or you'll get hurt."

That was the advice my brother Matthew gave me when he introduced me to varsity football. He had played organized football for years and was very good at it. So when I told him I wanted to play, just before he graduated, he connected me to the varsity coach. Matthew was also one of my coaches and personal trainer for football and wrestling. He taught me everything he knew, and he was also able to identify my strengths and coached me on how to use them to my advantage.

Football was the perfect sport for me. It was dangerous, a gladiator sport of athletics, but it was easy compared to life in the ghetto. Nothing was more dangerous than the ghetto. I was a running back and a strong safety. I was really the hitter on defense, which meant I got to hit people as hard as I wanted without getting into any trouble.

I started training with the juniors and seniors on the varsity team just before I started high school. Training was rigorous! That's where I learned how to hit and have people cheer for me at the same time. Football was an answer to a prayer I never prayed, a way for me to deal with the seeds of violence that had been planted in the crevices of my heart growing up. It was also a way for me to keep busy and stay out of trouble.

The streets were still calling, and sometimes they would come knocking on my front door. Drug dealers set up shop right in front of my house, and they were always ready to talk to the next potential employee. The conversations are just different on the street. But I wasn't interested in that kind of deviant entrepreneurship. There was nothing in it but money that grew wings and flew away and the possibility of me getting my own wings the hard way.

Those inner impressions kept getting stronger. Something in me was saying *You gotta go! You gotta do something else! You gotta do more to stay out of trouble, stay out of this life and this environment.* So, I did whatever it took to stay busy.

One of my older brothers, Marvin, was working at a temporary job. Normally, he would have a partner with him, but the partner left, so my brother was looking for someone to work with him. I was only sixteen at the time, and this was a night shift job, but I did not let that stop me from putting my bid in. The conversation was short and to the point.

"Hey, let me work with you."

"No. You're not old enough."

But I had bulldog tenacity, and once I set my mind on doing something, I was going to find a way. I came up with another plan and went to one of my other brothers, Marshall, and pitched my idea.

"Man, I've got to work! I need to get this job! Whyon't you let me use your ID?"

My brother eyed me, but before he could get a chance to answer, I went for the close.

"I've *got* to work, man! You know what they say, man: *all Black people look alike.*"

I really believed it would work, and I guess I had convinced him because he let me use his ID. We did not look exactly alike, but either it was close enough for me to pass or the employer only cared about putting a body in the spot. Whatever it was, I got the job.

I worked night shift for most of my high school years, getting up early for school, trying to stay awake in class, then going to football practice after school. I would leave football practice around five and take the long walk home to get there around five-thirty. I had to be at work at ten o'clock, so on a good day, I might get maybe three hours of sleep, and then rush out the house to get on the bus. I would work the graveyard shift from ten to six the next morning loading and unloading trailers, come home, try to get a couple hours of sleep and then make it to school. It was rough! I missed my first class almost every time.

Somewhere in there, I managed to squeeze wrestling into my schedule. I wrestled through the winter months, and then by the Spring, it was back to preconditioning for football. I stayed busy, and that's what helped me stay out of trouble. I had to stay busy because I knew the odds favored me being in the wrong place at the wrong time, and the street life was always just outside the door. Most of the people on the football team were in gangs. The high school was in our territory, but the practice field was in opps territory, and they did not care. They did not care if police were there. They did not care if coaches were there. They looked for the right opportunity to kill somebody.

Football kept me busy, but it wasn't safe by a longshot. We needed a battle strategy just for practice. Fortunately, our coach was from the 'hood. He had gone to the same high school as I did, so he was very familiar with the area. He knew all about the gangs and the thug life, so he would keep up with what was going on, and before every practice, he would make a decision about where we would meet. There was no planning in advance; it was a situation where you just dealt with it and took it day by day. I pushed my body to its limits at work, and then pushed it beyond those limits at practice. Day in and day out, that was my routine until I experienced what I call my defining moment.

It was the start of the football season my senior year in high school. We were practicing in a gym that day. Because of the gang wars, it wasn't safe for us to be at Fuller Park. Turf was the prize the gangs were fighting for, and there was a lot of retaliation going back and forth. There wasn't a whole lot we could do inside because we were limited by space, so we were running the stairs on the bleachers doing warmups. We ran up one side of the stairs, all the way to the top, across to the other side, down the stairs, and then back around. That was the routine. I had worked the night before and I was exhausted, but I kept running the stairs.

THE BIRTH OF DISCIPLINE

The graveyard shift was taking its toll on me. I was getting very little sleep, plus I wasn't eating right – junk food here and there throughout the school day – and I was just dragging. The other kids would slow down as soon as they thought the coach wasn't looking. By then, I was captain of the football team, and I was doing my best to lead by example, but I was just on the verge of giving up. I was barely trotting, about to start walking, but I kept running around, giving it all I had.

Everything hurt. Thoughts flooded my mind, and I rehearsed my day as if trying to convince my body it had done enough. *You got on the bus around eight o'clock, made it to the North side of Chicago, started work at ten, got off at six, home around seven, two hours of sleep.* All of that was running through my mind. My willingness to set the example was rapidly succumbing to the overwhelming reality of fatigue. *You have got to be crazy! You only got two hours sleep, overslept, and missed your first class like you aways do.*

My body tuned into my thoughts the way a skeptic tunes into a master hypnotist. My legs felt heavier, like wading through a sea of weights. My steps got slower, and my head bowed as my focus and energy shifted to the floor. Just when I felt I couldn't go any further, my coach screamed at me from across the gym.

"How bad do you want it, Bay? Huh? How bad do you want it, son?"

My head snapped to attention, and in that moment, his question became more about my life than running around a gym. That's when it hit me. Football wasn't just a sport I was good at; it was my ticket to get out. Thoughts were welling up on the inside. *I don't know where this ticket is going to take me, but I'm going to get out!*

I had been running the bleachers for about thirty minutes or more, and as I started down the stairs, my lungs were on fire. My chest was tightening with every breath, and my legs felt like they were giving out. I could feel my muscles tensing and cramping, but Coach's words shot through me like a supercharged adrenaline rush. I never said a word, I didn't have to because my whole being responded, and suddenly, I knew I wanted that ticket out more than anything.

I took off so fast, I shocked myself! We were supposed to be doing a hard jog, but I took off sprinting up and down the bleachers. I don't remember how many times I went. I knew about getting your second wind; I've had that experience on more than one occasion. But this was beyond that. Fresh air rushed through my entire being seemingly out of nowhere. I felt superhuman – that's the best way I can describe it. How it happened, I can't tell you. To this day, I don't understand it.

That day, I discovered a me I never knew. That's when I realized that there is something inside that can override external factors. Even when everything is working against you, there's a living, breathing, better version of yourself inside your body that is powerful enough to take over when you physically, mentally, and emotionally just want to give up. There was a me I could not see that stood up and introduced himself that day. It was as though he walked up to me and said, *I'll take it from here.*

There's a kind of hopelessness that comes from being beat down when all you're trying to do is be better and change is hard to find. The gravelly sound of disappointment and failure can wear away your hopes and dreams until all that's left is a well-worn groove where they used to be or could have been. You feel trapped in a body that is slotted by powers seen and

THE BIRTH OF DISCIPLINE

unseen to be yet another statistic. Then just when it looks like the vertigo of rapid descent threatens to drop you six feet in defeat, the unsealed casket bursts open in a Lazarus moment and the "inner me" comes out from under, grave clothes and all.

How bad do you want it? My mind was made up. I was going to let this inner me take charge and focus on what he wanted, even if it meant making my body a slave to his desires. I had felt the power of his momentum, and like a mind that is stretched by a new experience, I knew I could not undo what had been done. I had learned the rigors of physical training, but this was a different kind of commitment to discipline. It started with a decision, then a conviction. *This is the way, this is how I'm going to get there, and this is what I'm going to do.* If football was my way out, nothing was going to stop me. I would keep at it despite the obstacles, despite the trials, despite the situation. I teamed up with my inner me and gave my all to football.

I set my sights on the NFL, and I went hard all the way up to my senior year in high school. Between work and football, there was absolutely no play for me. New habits were forming, and then those habits began to form me. Before each football game, I would go into a corner by myself. Even though I had seen Mama pray countless times, and aside from that encounter in the closet, I did not know how to pray on my own. The only prayer I felt confident saying was the "Our Father, who art in Heaven ..." prayer that my grandmother taught me.

I would go into a corner and say that prayer under my breath so no one could hear me. Then I would meditate on it, turning it over in my mind and saying the words quietly to myself. Then I would meditate on what I was going to do in the football game, rehearsing what I wanted and expected to happen.

The inner me was more welcoming of the strong impressions. When he felt like picking up a Bible and reading it, I went with it. It still felt strange, and I still couldn't understand what I was reading, but I did it anyway. I still struggled with my grades. I even had to sit out football during my sophomore year because of it. But for the first time in my life, I felt I had found a way to prove that I was not a failure. I played so well in my senior year, I was selected to play in the all-star game. I was an arrow aimed at a target, and at the rate I was going, I did not see how I could miss.

Things were finally starting to look up. I was one of the fortunate few who got to my senior year in high school in one piece. I had never been gang jumped or even grazed with a bullet. I was an all-star player by day, and still loading trucks on the docks at night. Part of my job involved guiding the truck drivers into the loading bays. I had done it so many times, I could do it in my sleep.

One day, I was guiding a driver who was backing into a very tight spot. Normally, I would back them into a dock, but this was one of those small locations where they didn't have an actual dock, just a garage door. So it was my job to back him up to the door. I had done this hundreds of times for at least a year. I knew the routine so well, I could do it half asleep. But because this particular bay was so narrow, to get the truck backed up to the door, it had to be perfect with maybe a half of an inch between the truck and the walls on each side. It was tight!

I had to guide this driver so he didn't damage the building by hitting the brick walls. I was on the driver's side directing him.

"Come back. Come back."

It was almost second nature for me because I had been doing it for so long. I knew exactly how close he could back up before I needed to signal for him to stop. Everything looked good, and I'm watching the wall while I'm directing him.

"Okay, come back. Come back."

It looked like we were going to get this truck backed in perfectly, but this driver was so excited that he stopped paying attention to me. Now he was looking at the side mirror on the passenger side.

"Come back. Come— Hold! Hold! Hold! Whoa!"

Before I realized what happened, I could hear the dull crunch of my arm being smashed against the brick wall as searing hot pain shot through my body. My other hand went up instinctively as if to locate where the pain was coming from, but it was useless. The pinch point was already cutting off the blood flow and numbness created a sense of dismemberment. I felt disoriented like I was searching in the dark trying to feel where my arm was supposed to be. But all I found in its place was what felt like jolts of burning hot electricity.

By now the truck driver had inched the truck forward, and I stumbled forward clutching my mangled arm. He shut off the truck, jumped out of his cab, and ran over to where I was.

"How is it? It looks like it's broken."

I was groaning. "Yeah, I'm in pain!"

"Can you move it? Can you move it?"

The most I could get out was groans. He ran and got some ice from a nearby gas station and rushed me into the warehouse half swearing, half trying to explain what happened. The office staff responded as though he had just told them about the next delivery.

"Oh, we can't do nothing. He's not even our employee. He's a temporary worker so he has to go through his agency."

The pain was excruciating! My arm locked against my chest, frozen at a ninety-degree angle as if being held up in an invisible sling. It remained that way for the next six months.

The injury was worse than a break because the muscles and tendons were completely crushed. The doctors hadn't seen anything like it. The physical therapy that followed was nearly as painful as the injury itself. Two to three times a week I endured torture as the therapists massaged the broken muscles trying to coax them out of their rigor mortis-like state. Time was going by, and my arm did not seem to be getting any better. I missed the all-star game. My arm succumbed to the trauma of the accident and all movement died taking my dreams of playing in the NFL with it.

By the time my high school graduation rolled around, my arm was dangling at my side. Mama was all smiles in her pink dress and her Sunday best hat. It made me happy to see her smile, and I was equally as happy just to graduate, but I was filled with mixed emotions. Deep down inside, I knew that my work-related injury guaranteed an end to what I saw as my only shot at something better in life.

Things began to go downhill from there. A thick, dark blanket of depression came over me. *I can't work. I'm not college material. What am I supposed to do now?* Football was all I had. I knew I wasn't good at academics, so I had pegged all my dreams on sports. I didn't need to have good grades to play football. I just needed to get by.

They say never put all your eggs in one basket, but what do you do when you only have one egg? A dream without the will to consistently fight for it is a dead dream. As my thoughts turned inward, hopelessness was suffocating me. Every now and then I would sense faith from that small dark closet tapping me on the shoulder telling me to take a step and do something. But God knew I didn't believe in myself, and even if I wanted to do something, I did not know what to do or how. I needed help.

SEVEN
THE SUBTLE VOICE OF FAITH

You see the old way wasn't working, so it's on us to do what we gotta do to survive.

I had never read an entire book. I could barely read, couldn't write a lick, spelling was horrible, and I barely made it out of high school. One of my teachers in her end-of-semester assessment said, "He really thinks. He's a thinker." I could barely spell my name, but I was a thinker. She nailed it, but thinking alone wasn't going to get me anywhere. I had done the bare minimum in my classes, just enough to keep me on the football team. I was convinced academics just wasn't my thing. Now, here I was, nineteen and just graduating from high school with no future in football to fall back on.

Mama encouraged me to register at a junior college with my younger sister, Matilda. I did not have the confidence, desire, or even the will to do it for myself. I was still the boy who looked in the mirror and saw nothing looking back at me. I saw very little value in myself, but I would do just about anything for

Mama if I thought it could make her life better. *Yeah, I'll do it for Mama.* If I could somehow make her life better, it would be worth it. Plus I was tired of living in the graveyard of my dreams. So, I decided to take that step.

All through high school, I scraped by doing just enough to move from one grade to the next. Now that I didn't have athletics to lean on anymore, the only way I was going to get into this college was to take a placement test. What happens when a kid believes he has learning disabilities and barely passing was all that was required to participate in high school sports? The way I saw it, I had two options. I could become yet another statistic and disappear into the sea of maybes and if only's of unfulfilled potential. Or, I could stand on my own fence and make myself visible, persevering like my father did against the odds of almost certain rejection.

I determined to stick to my decision to apply for college even if going after a better future meant exposing my past failures. I took the placement test, and the truth came out. I tested at a seventh-grade level. I was starting at the bottom, and the voices of failure came roaring back.

Moraine Valley Community College was out in the suburbs of Southwest Chicago away from the noise and distractions of the inner-city community that I knew so well. I started out commuting from the South Side to Palos Heights, Illinois, about an hour and a half round trip on the bus. Eventually, Mama and DD rented an apartment for me and my sister closer to the school to save on out-of-district tuition cost.

It was in a place called Justice, Illinois, a predominantly White area. That was a major culture shock for me since I had lived in a predominantly Black, inner-city ghetto all my life. Moving to this new community with its picture-perfect single-family homes and manicured lawns was a whole new world. I entered it with the same thinking that I was accustomed to in my old neighborhood, not realizing that you cannot use old tactics when you're facing a new enemy. But Mama knew.

"Bay-Bay, don't walk out at night."

"Aw, Ma. It's okay. This ain't nothin' compared to the 'hood."

I was twenty years old, living almost on my own and feeling my grown self. I figured Mama was just doing what mothers do.

"Ain't nothin' go'n happen to me. Ain't no crime out here like around our house."

Mama did not say another word.

I had lived twenty years of my life and managed to dodge every bullet. What could possibly happen to me out here in this squeaky clean, cookie-cutter neighborhood? I knew what I was doing, and I felt confident that there could be nothing as bad here as where I was coming from, but boy, was I mistaken!

There was a road right in front of the apartment complex, just beyond the parking lot. I walked out of my apartment building one night and was heading across the parking lot, minding my own business. Just then, a car full of kids was driving by and they lowered the window.

"NIG-GER! NIGGER! NIGGER! NIG-GER!"

In my community, you could sense trouble. You could sense the opposite gang. In many cases, they didn't even have to wear the paraphernalia or use the symbols or anything like that. You just knew. Gangs fought over turf. They retaliated when those they considered their enemies attacked. Right or wrong, you could at least make sense of it. But this gang was more dangerous. There was no logic, no excuse for retaliation, no territory to take over.

In that moment, I realized I had left one gang-infested community for another. I was hated here, not because of a gang or what one opps member did to another opps member, or because I had killed someone. They simply hated me for my color, and their hatred was palpable.

I turned around and headed back towards the apartment. I wasn't afraid, but I felt so frustrated and confused, I did not know what else to do. I understood the gang thing and the drugs. I understood that as clear as day. But until that moment, I realized I was clueless as to what goes on in the world outside of my community. Here I was doing what I thought was right and what I could do to get away from the violence only to be confronted by it in a different and more volatile form.

The irony of living in a place called Justice stung worse than a hard, wet slap in the face. *Is this what I clawed my way out of the ghetto for?* A transfusion was taking place, but instead of something new, healthy, and life-giving being pumped into my system, it was as though my hopes of a better life were being drained out of me, and the old fight-your-way-out mentality was being pumped back in, filling every cell with despair and hopelessness.

I'mma go back to the 'hood! I'mma round up as many thugs as I can, then I'm gonna come back out here and just ramshack the place! My mind was in an uproar. But then the inner me tried to reason. *Do you really want to do that? What is that going to get you? Why are you here anyway?*

There was a real battle going on in my mind. Whatever decision I made was about to change everything. Do I give in to the old mindset and forfeit everything that brought me this far? Or do I face the reality of racism head-on and do what I came here to do in spite of it? I thought about Mama. I thought about all the punishment I had put my body through working, training, doing everything just to stay out of trouble. I thought about my smashed arm and my shredded ticket of NFL dreams. Perseverance and determination had gotten me this far. I decided to see how much further it would take me.

It was not easy going to school with predominantly white people. I was in a different kind of opps territory, and there would be nobody from my neighborhood waiting to meet me at the boulevard to make sure I got home safely. I had to learn to be independent knowing there were a lot of people at the college who hated me because of my skin color. Racial slurs being yelled out of an open car window was only one of my concerns. I still needed to confront the goliath that defeated me in academics my entire life, and I needed money to finance my warfare.

My first two years at college were a surreal mixture of frustration and hoping against hope. The inner me felt like I was supposed to be there, but everything else was screaming the results of a losing battle through the megaphone of my mind. *School is not for me. I'm a kid from the 'hood, and we don't do school. We don't do reading. We don't do studying. We don't do any of that.* But no matter what I told myself, something kept me going back the next day and the day after that.

I blamed everything on God. That was the only way I could make sense of this pull I felt to keep pushing forward. At the same time, I questioned Him because I could not understand why He would see anything in me. It had to be Him that led me here, but why would He lead me to college, and why *this* college? I could not understand it, but the inner me seemed convinced He wanted me there. Graduation wasn't even my goal – that was too far ahead and felt like too big of a target. My focus was on getting through each day, and I was struggling big time.

My grades quickly took the slippery slope downward. I went to my professors for help, but as far as they were concerned, if I couldn't cut it, I didn't belong there. When the familiar D's and F's started showing up, I went to my teachers to let them know I was diagnosed with learning disabilities. I tried to explain how hard it was for me to catch on.

"Is there anything you can do for me?"

Each time I asked the question, it was met with the same deadpan response.

"Maybe they shouldn't have taken you out of the learning disability classes in sixth grade. Maybe they should have kept you in there. I think it would have helped you."

That was their typical way of letting me know, *you're just not getting it, so I can't help you.* Their verbal shrug was a signal that there was nothing further to discuss and an excuse to let me know that I did not belong there in a way that posed no threat to their tenure.

It's one thing to not want help, but it's a whole other scenario when you're practically begging for help, and no one seems to give a care. I felt sorry for myself since no one else would. Not that I wanted pity, but I was hoping someone would care enough to at least point me in the right direction. I kept telling myself that it was all God's fault. He's the one who made me want more without giving me a clear way to get it. Surely He must know He made a big mistake.

I felt alienated all over again. It was a déjà vu experience reminiscent of my days back in elementary school. I was the kid who was seen as dirty with hair and clothes that did not look like everybody else's. I became a loner, but this time I wasn't forced there because no one welcomed me. This time, I chose to be there. I was struggling, but deep down inside, I knew that staying in school was what I needed to do. It felt like I was being led to be there. That frustrated the living daylights out of me because I was on a path where I was failing, but I knew I needed to stay on that path, and I hated it. I *hated* it.

The inner me and the shell-shocked, battle-weary me were at odds every single day. I stumbled from one class to the next, pretending to be an engaged member of the college community, never knowing when I would step on the next academic landmine. And then, as if through the dense smoke of freshly fired artillery, I spied a foxhole, a program for adults who had been out of school for a long time.

This program was offered at the college, and the classes were designed to help you get back on track. My classmates were predominantly White students in their upper fifties, most of them with families. I was the only young person in there, and I knew I had to do three to four times more than the average person because they could retain and understand the material and I could not. But I did not let that stop me. No one was going to give me a free pass. I had to do what I had to do to get where I needed to go.

The classes were mostly memorization, which made it a little easier for me because the teachers used more visuals. But whenever they would get more technical or stick strictly with the textbook where I had to study, I would be completely lost. I was taking it one day at a time. Instead of trying to learn, I tried to remember everything. I would sit in the lectures and just barely comprehend anything. Afterwards, I would come back to my apartment with all these textbooks, and I would literally cry from frustration.

My apartment became the closet of my younger years.

"God, if You're real, please help me."

Once again, I found myself crying out in desperation and the heavens responding with stony silence.

"I don't understand this thing. I have no idea why You got me here. It's like I'm talking to a brick wall. I can't do this!"

That became my routine. School, frustration, running back to my apartment and begging God to help me. I did not know if God actually spoke to ordinary people like me, but I was hoping for something, *anything*! I never heard an audible voice, but it was as though the inner me kept saying *stick to it*, but I did not believe I could do it. I was stuck on a hamster wheel of defeat, wearing myself out trying so hard but never getting anywhere. Then I would find myself back on my knees praying, asking God to take away this pull I felt to be at school, or give me something else.

"Open my mind or something. Or, better yet, come down from the clouds and talk to me. Teach me. Change my life!"

I was failing. Algebra was the only class I was passing, and that was because the teacher used a more visual approach and broke things down to a junior high school level. There was just something about the way he taught that allowed me to grasp the basic concepts. But in everything else, I was officially flunking out of college, and Language Arts was the worst!

I tried to read the textbook, but I could not comprehend anything. Nothing! Sometimes I would sit and try to read for two hours at a time, but I would not remember one thing, not even the thing I had just read five minutes earlier. I would find myself praying, *God, why do you have me here? What hope is there?* Then one day, I got an answer, but not the one I was looking for.

I had just finished what had become my new daily workout, praying for an hour or two until I got tired. I mean, I would be sweating bricks, I would be praying so hard. All of a sudden, I sensed this impression on the inside.

Read the Bible.

It was a strong impression, like the inner me was having a conversation with the invisible God Mama used to write letters to. But that did not change the fact that I could barely read and did not understand anything when I did try to read. *What would be the point of reading the Bible?*

I would read three chapters and not understand one word of it. So, I would pray again, but now the impression would be a little stronger. I wanted God to talk to me, but I really did not know if that was even possible. He talked to Mama, at least she acted like He did, but that was different. She was a prayer warrior, not a struggling student. I started to wonder about this "voice" I was hearing. *Was it just me wanting to believe I was hearing something? Why am I feeling this way? Why does it feel like God is saying something? It had to be God talking, right?* I chose to believe that it was because the only other explanation would be that I was losing my mind.

Read the Bible.

I sensed the words so clearly that it was as though I had heard an audible voice. I could not read a textbook. How would reading the Bible help me? *He's telling me to read this thing, but I don't know what I'm reading.* No matter how much I tried to reason my way out of it, I could not shake the clarity of the impression.

"Okay, I'll do it!" I spit the words out. "I can't understand anything, but I'm gonna do what You say. But this is stupid!"

I picked up the Bible to begin to try to read, and it happened again. I heard the voice even clearer than before.

Before you read, say this.

I responded to what I was hearing before I had a chance to process what I was doing and said the words I was told to pray.

"Father, I don't understand what's in this book. Therefore, I'm trusting You to teach me anyhow. So, teach me Your word."

Then I read the Bible, still not understanding anything on the pages. After I finished reading, I went back to the textbook. Nothing! But now it wasn't on me. Now it's on Him. It was His responsibility to teach me. He's telling me to read this thing and it's His responsibility to teach me. As far as I was concerned, I was doing my part. I made up my mind that I would keep reading it. I would not even try to understand it. I was done with trying to understand it now.

I started saying a simple prayer every day. *Lord, I thank You for teaching me Your word.* That was it. Then I would pick up where I left off and begin to read, chapter by chapter. Still nothing, no comprehension whatsoever. But it wasn't my problem anymore. *If I don't get it, that's not my fault. That's Your problem.*

Day after day it was the same. Struggle in class, go back to the apartment, pray and read the Bible, then read the textbook. I did not know if I was doing it out of dogged determination or flat-out desperation, but that became my pattern for dealing with my failure at school. Midterms came and went, and nothing changed. Final exams were approaching, and nothing seemed to be changing. I would pick up the textbook, and I could not understand it any more than the time before that and the time before that.

I stopped being polite with God and just started railing at Him in frustration, an hour, sometimes two hours, just hollering at God. But no matter how exasperated I became, the impression would be the same.

Read the Bible.

I would snatch the Bible up, whip it open and start reading. Then from the Bible, I would go to my textbook. I'd wake up the next day, and it was fresh and new. All the stress and heartache and pain and frustration of the previous day would be gone. But when I got to school and I could not comprehend anything, it would start all over again.

But all of a sudden, things just started to click. It started with the Bible first. One day I picked it up and tried to read like I had done many times before, but this time, I started to understand what I was reading. It was like a Helen Keller moment when she finally made the connection between the words Anne Sullivan signed in the palm of her hand and the reality the word represented. I started to understand what the words meant. After reading the Bible, I picked up my textbook and I started comprehending the subject matter.

That was the pattern or cycle, over and over with each class and each lesson. If I was frustrated with content, I would pray. God would say, *read the Bible*, and I would read. It was as if someone was shining a light in my mind, and I would begin to understand things. I began to understand, and even though I did not see or recognize it at the time, that built confidence in me. After reading the Bible – which in my mind was more complicated than *anything* else I ever read – I would pick up my textbooks expecting to understand something rather than expecting defeat.

For the first two years of college, it was just like that. Now that I think about it, my prayers even changed after I began to read the Bible. They became more intimate. It wasn't just begging and pleading. It was more of a conversation with a trusted confidante or tutor. I began to thank God for giving me understanding rather than complaining. The Bible became like food to me. I hardly ever said grace over a plate of actual food, but I would say my grace over the Bible before reading just like some people say their grace or a prayer over their food before eating. The more I did that, the more things changed on the inside. I was developing what I call *sticktoitiveness*.

I remember having to write a five-page paper for my Language Arts class. You might as well have been asking me to write Moby Dick! I did the best I could and handed it in. I was already devising a plan to try to work with the teacher to see what I could do to make up the grade. I hated getting my work graded. I had seen enough D's and F's, so when the teacher passed out our papers, I took mine and automatically approached her desk. I had my rote speech prepared. *I have problems with reading and writing.* Etcetera, etcetera, same old story. I stood a respectful distance away from the teacher's desk and started my plea.

"Is there anything else I could do, any type of program or tutoring or anything like that?"

I'll never forget the look on her face. It was a strange combination of surprise and slight annoyance.

"Did you see your grade?"

I glanced at the paper. I saw the grade, but I did not see the name.

"Oh yeah, I saw it."

She paused before continuing. "I'll see what we have, but I don't think you need it."

With that, she shook her head slightly and turned her attention back to what she was doing. I just assumed she was slightly annoyed at having to even address what I presumed was an obvious need. But then it clicked, right then it clicked. *Wait a minute. Did I hear her correctly?* Here was a teacher telling me that she didn't think I needed help. I stared at the glaring red A on the white page, and it began to sink in. *Oh my God! This is more than me just understanding some words in a book. I am really understanding this stuff now!*

You know, you can get so used to failure that you can fail to recognize when change has come. It was as though I had been reading in the dark all this time and someone finally turned on a bright light so I could make out what was on the pages. It all started to click just like that. The D's and F's started to change to A's and B's, and I started passing everything.

As my GPA improved, my confidence gradually started building up, and I dared to raise my head and look beyond just the next step. I finally had a strategy, something I could do about failure, disappointment, and defeat. I was building muscles inside me just as sure as running around the gym and working out used to build my body. This was a new exercise regimen, but it was spiritual rather than physical.

My relationship with God began to change. He had not been ignoring me all this time. He had been training me, helping me to exercise the muscles of persistence and what I now came to recognize as faith – acting on what He told me to do. Now I felt Him leading me day by day. It was as though He was trying to get through this thick skull of mine to convince me to believe that He really was rooting for me. He was showing me that He could be trusted even when what He was saying did not make any sense to me. And day by day, when I thought He was just frustrating me, He was really being patient with me, testing my mettle the way a good coach does.

"How bad do you want it, son?"

I went from failing to a 3.5 GPA that semester. I swapped my old workout for a new one and developed a new discipline. Instead of running laps after school as I did in high school, I ran back to my apartment to pray, read the Bible and study. For the first time in my life, I felt truly courageous, and this was not the false bravado of the streets that hides behind fists or some other kind of weapon. This was coming from the inner me, from the sense of knowing that I had Someone invincible in my corner. He did not care that I came from the South Side. He did not care what color my skin was. He only cared about helping me to succeed.

EIGHT
THE ROAD TO BECOMING UNCONQUERABLE

Don't believe everything you hear: real eyes, realize, real lies.

Knowledge can be like a diagnosis of a terminal disease, like cancer. A person can be walking around feeling fine, go to the doctor for a regular checkup, and the doctor all of a sudden says, "We found a lump." The person never felt the lump, but now the expert is telling them that they have stage four cancer. They were walking around feeling fine, but as soon as they got the diagnosis, the knowledge they have of cancer becomes the thing that dominates their thinking. They start to act and feel like they have stage 4 cancer. They stop trying to live and start preparing to die, and before they know it, they're gone. It makes you wonder, was it the cancer that took the person out or the knowledge of it?

The biggest enemy to success is not trying and failing. It can be the knowledge you choose to believe as the truth. That knowledge can stop you dead in your tracks because it can keep you from trying. This was a lesson I was about to learn the hard way.

I was riding on a high. I had made a major accomplishment by not becoming a normal statistic associated with my background. Despite all odds, given I had to start over, I was on my way to finishing junior college. Granted, what should have taken me two years under normal circumstances took me nearly four years when it was all said and done. But I was still on my way to graduating.

My little sister, Matilda, had once again passed me. She finished in the expected two years and went on to bigger and better things. By then, I had a car of my own, thanks to my older brother. And with Matilda gone, there was no reason for me to hang around on campus, so I would go back to the apartment between classes.

One day, after I went back to the apartment, while I was waiting until it was time to go back for my next class, I turned the TV on. I started flipping through the channels, and just so happened to see Oprah Winfrey. I did not normally watch Oprah. On occasion, she would talk about something that interested me enough to tune in, but touchy-feely type shows just weren't for me. However, this time, she had a guest who was talking about something that caught my attention.

I tuned in because some of what the expert was describing sounded a lot like what I had experienced in my life. He called it *dyslexia*. To be honest, most of what he was talking about sounded like a foreign language to me. But every now and then, a familiar word or phrase would filter through – "difficulty reading and interpreting what was read," "struggling with comprehension."

He talked about difficulty recognizing words which causes people with dyslexia to have a hard time learning. He went on to talk about the various kinds of dyslexia, the most severe, in his opinion, being "double-deficit" dyslexia, the category most prevalent with weak readers. This particular form of dyslexia had a double-whammy effect because it caused the person to have trouble recognizing words, which in turn made them have a hard time learning and memorizing words.

With all he said, there was one familiar phrase that was interjected over and over, one with which I was very familiar: *learning disorder*. Even if I did not know anything else the guy was talking about, I knew a *lot* about learning disorders. That was a label I had worn like a badge of shame all through my academic years. I remember thinking, *man, that's what I got.* The more I internalized the thought that I had dyslexia, the more I started to feel like there was no hope for me. *I'm not like everybody else.*

I remember hearing a story about a man who had been broke so long, the only places he could afford to live were section-8 type government subsidized housing. Every month, he would feel traumatized when the landlord was coming to collect because he knew he did not have enough money to pay. When he finally started making a lot of money, he bought a beautiful mansion. His impoverished past was behind him, but the knowledge of it was still embedded in his psyche.

One day, he woke out of a deep sleep to a knock on the door. He was in a panic because he woke up thinking it was the landlord. In his drowsy stupor, he flashed back to his past, thinking he did not have enough to pay the landlord. He jumped out of the bed and was almost halfway to the bathroom before he realized he *was* the landlord.

Your past can be like that sometimes. It can creep up on you when you least expect it and convince you that you are still in the same place you used to be even when you are far from it. That is what happened to me when I heard that expert talking. I was not struggling in my classes at the time. I was not drifting off in classes anymore. Yes, I was in my third year at a two-year junior college, but I was understanding the material and finally getting A's and B's in all my classes. But in that moment, listening to that expert, I heard a certain knowledge that I accepted as truth.

The old familiar feeling of frustration crept over me, and all the excitement of my recent academic triumphs drained out of me, leaving my insides as white as a sheet. All of a sudden, my recent academic experiences were overridden by one word, *dyslexia*. Hearing it made me feel like I had been told I had a terminal disease, and I had accepted the diagnosis. I convinced myself that all of my success was just a freakish accident. *Yeah it was just a fluke. I'm not smart. How could I be when I have dyslexia?* The moment I accepted that knowledge as my truth, everything went downhill. Confidence drained out of me, and depression became my shadowy companion.

It just so happened the following weekend, I went home to visit Mama. I walked into the second living room where she was sitting and slumped down on the couch next to her.

"Hey, Mama."

She had my baby niece balanced across her knees, swaying her from side to side and patting her on the back, lulling her to sleep.

"Hey, Bay-Bay." It was as though she could feel the weight of my depression and discouragement sitting next to her. "What's going on, son?"

"Mama, I was watching Oprah, and you know what, I think I got dyslexia. You know what I mean?"

Mama's knees stopped swaying, but she was still patting away. I continued.

"I've always wondered why I failed at school and stuff like that, why I wasn't doing well in school, but I think I have dyslexia."

As I started to explain my symptoms, Mama whipped her head around, angled her body towards me, and looked me right in the eyes. I recognized that look. It was the same take-no-prisoners expression she would get on her face when she was about to deal with anything she deemed as evil behavior. I knew beyond any shadow of a doubt that she meant business. When we were younger, if she had a belt or switch in her hand and you saw that look on her face, you knew you were about to get it!

She pursed her lips, and her body shook as she spoke.

"No, you don't! And don't you *ever* say that again! That devil is a *liar!*"

Her reaction was so quick and forceful, she startled me, and she wasn't finished with her rebuke.

"Your last grades were A's and B's! Now here come the devil trying to sneak in, telling you you got a disability. Don't you *ever* say that again! That devil is a *liar!*"

Now, she completely overlooked the fact that I used to consistently get D's and F's. She refused to consider that.

"This semester you got A's and B's, now here's this devil trying to sneak in!"

When she said that I thought, *wait a minute, I did get A's, and I understand the material.*

Mama spoke as if the devil had been put on trial. Now she was ready to make her closing argument.

"From this day forward, *every day*, you tell God 'I thank you for giving me a *brilliant* mind!'"

She looked away and went back to swaying her knees a little more vigorously than before and continued patting my niece back to sleep. I could feel tears making tracks down my face. I heard Mama loud and clear, but I still felt confused. I had been thoroughly convinced I had dyslexia, but Mama said I did not.

It matters whose words you believe. You have to decide whose words you are going to allow to be the "expert" opinion in your life. Whose report will you believe? I chose to believe the words of the woman who had done nothing but love and nurture me all my life. It took a few days for what she said to really take root, but when it did, it was all golden. I finished my last two years and graduated with a 2.5 average. I may not have been in the top of my class, but I knew for sure I was *not* stupid or dyslexic.

Failure is an event, not a person. That's why you will never be a failure. Don't believe the lies and the labels that people who don't know anything about who you really are try to put on you. And if you don't have someone like my mama to tell you the truth, you've got to tell it to yourself. Even if you do have someone to encourage you, you've still got to tell yourself, because at the end of the day, the words that carry the most weight are the ones *you* say.

Every day, tell yourself the person you want to be. Like my mother told me to tell myself, "I have a brilliant mind," decide what you need to say, and say it as though it's true *now*. Say, "I am," not "I will be." Even if you don't believe it at first, keep saying it anyway. Eventually, you *will* believe, and that's when everything will begin to change.

I had leaped over another hurdle and broken through one of the biggest barricades in my mind. I was not stupid. I was not learning disabled. I was not an ignorant, hopeless case. I had made the right choice in deciding whose voice to tune into. The fact is, sometimes teachers fall into the rut of doing the bare minimum too, and the experts are not expert on the subject of you. I was learning. It takes strength and determination to neutralize all the negativity the world throws at us in the media, in the classroom, and as I was soon to discover, in the workplace.

My father's words always stayed with me. "The only thing that comes to a lazy man is a dream." I wasn't looking for any handouts in Justice, Illinois. I knew I had to work. So, I got a job at Target Greatland, the chain that eventually became Super Target stores. Initially, my schedule was all over the place. But I eventually got a fixed schedule where I worked ten hours a day, four days a week. I was in school full-time and working full-time, and it was extremely difficult. I would drive over to Hodgkins, Illinois, pull up in the lot, look up at the red bullseye next to "Target" with "Greatland" in green script underneath, and head inside the warehouse-like building where I would be harassed for the next few years.

I worked my way up to team lead, which meant I was third on the totem pole under managers and executive managers, with the store manager sitting in top position. The store manager was a German guy, 6'4" and about 300-pounds. And while he could not do it physically, let's just say he found ways to throw his weight around, and I became his target.

"Hey! So, what you guys do, man? You B-lack folks. What you guys do?" Or, "Yeah, so, I'm German. We gas folks." I had to deal with crazy comments like that just about every day. Fortunately for me and for him, I had started developing my relationship with God, and that was when things began to change drastically for me. I started to become more sensitive to what I grew to recognize as the voice of God. Those impressions that I sensed on the inside were Him all along. There was no booming thunderous voice coming out of Heaven, just a calm, quiet guiding from within. After the expert-on-Oprah incident, I came to rely more heavily on that inner voice. He was in my corner for sure, and I was open to and focused on doing whatever He wanted me to do. I trusted Him.

I had been spending more and more time reading the Bible and praying. It wasn't just about classes anymore. I had conversations with Him, and I knew that if I stuck with Him, I would get where I needed to go. I was convinced He wanted me at that college. And I started to believe that once I graduated, maybe I would go on the mission field or something like that. But for the time being, I was going to school full-time and working full-time.

I was working so hard that I had no time for church or any other social activities. In retail, fifty percent of the revenue comes in Friday through Sunday, and because I was a team lead, I had to work weekends. And that manager had me doing some crazy stuff – anything to try to provoke a reaction. He would call me from the stock room on the walkie-talkie, tell me to come to the break room, and then tell me to open the refrigerator

"Get down and clean this up! This is a mess in here!"

I could have easily gotten one of the employees that reported to me to do the ridiculous nit-picky stuff he was telling me to do, and there were janitors who could have done it. But I knew it was me he was after, so I kept the battle on my field.

In his eyes, I was guilty of being Black. And to rub salt in his wound, I was Black *and* a team lead. That meant I had been put in charge of an area and whoever worked in that area. It really stuck in his craw that this Black guy had non-Black people reporting to me, so he took every opportunity to try to demean me. I knew what he was doing, but I did not let it faze me because now I knew I had a purpose. I knew I was on my way somewhere, and I wasn't about to allow this guy to get to me. He was a distraction, and I knew it, so, I was determined to stay focused.

So, you know what I did? I cleaned the refrigerator while he stood over me, positioning his shoes close to my knees as if that was the posture I was meant to be in. Between smirks, he spit out instructions for how he wanted it cleaned and watched to make sure I did it exactly as he said.

One particular day, I looked up at him as I was cleaning and laughed.

"I can't wait man. I can't wait!"

He had this smug expression on his face, but he couldn't resist.

"Oh? Wait for what?"

I rubbed a little more vigorously and laughed again.

"I can't wait until I become the director and you report to me, and I have *you* cleaning this out."

He put all 300-something pounds behind his laugh.

"Okay. You think you get to become director?"

I had learned from Mama, how she kept quiet when she tried to warn me about what to expect when I moved to Justice. So I looked at him and smiled, and I didn't say another word. My silence must have really gotten under his skin because he started pushing me even harder after that, wasting my time doing menial tasks that he knew I wasn't supposed to be doing. Until one day, he crossed the line.

He strolled over, just close enough to get my attention. He always made a point to not dignify me by calling me by my name.

"Hey! Get that lift and put this pallet away."

If you did not know what you were doing, the lift could cause serious injury. And he knew that I was not trained to use that piece of equipment, but he made me use it anyway. He had direct access to people that made decisions, and he himself was a decision-maker. If I had gone against him, it would be my word against his. So, it was either do what he said, or risk losing my job.

Where he instructed me to put the pallet was a tough spot. I had to maneuver the lift and reorganize everything while he barked out orders telling me to do this and do that. I could tell he was enjoying watching me sweat. He stood there with his arms folded waiting for me to fail, but it wasn't quite the ending he had hoped for. I got the job done injury and damage-free.

I put the lift back with a big ol' grin on my face.

"Hey, how do you like it, man? Looks good."

"Yeah, yeah. Pretty good for a *Black* guy."

The look on his face was as though he could not believe he had actually said that out loud. I just looked at him and shook my head. He tried to clean it up, but it was like mopping a muddy floor with dirty water.

"Oh, you know I didn't mean that, right? I mean, you know, in a *derogatory* way."

The more he talked, the deeper a hole he dug for himself.

"But you're good, you know?"

He was really trying, but he was just making things worse. Now it was my turn to fold my arms and watch him sweat. I just kind of chuckled to myself as he kept talking.

"You know what, man? Imma tell you something, man. I have worked with a lot of Black people. But I will tell you one thing about Black people, man."

The irony was laughable. Here's a White German guy trying to convince me that he knew more about being Black than I did. Now this I had to hear!

He stumbled along, "Whatever you do, you don't call them out of their name, man. Oh, man! I mean they snap!"

I think the guy forgot what he had said just a few seconds earlier, and he must have definitely forgotten he was addressing one of the "them" he was talking about.

He finally came to a rolling stop. "But you don't seem to be like that."

I think he really believed he was giving me a compliment, or as close to a compliment as he was capable of. What he said made no sense whatsoever, and all I saw when I looked at this guy was a man who had set traps for me and used his authority as the bait.

Things took a strange twist after that incident. He went from one extreme to the other to the point where he started calling me his son. It was like something out of *The Twilight Zone*! He had flipped from the one who persecuted me to someone who patronized me. I did not like it, but I was learning to pick my battles. I kept reminding myself that I was on my way somewhere, and I refused to be detoured.

You have to be laser-focused and keep your eyes set on your future to get where you need to go. You might not be one hundred percent sure where that is yet, but you have to be disciplined, knowing that you are destined to get beyond any roadblocks, detours, or distractions. No matter what, deep down inside, know that there's a way around this thing, whatever "this thing" is. Be determined to come out on top.

For me, my focus was on graduating from junior college and then doing whatever came after that. I did not have time to worry about what my manager or anyone else's perceptions of me were or what preconceived stereotypes they had. I already knew that being a Black man in America was considered by many to be a disadvantage. I had already escaped the "learning disability" label, and I refused to be "disadvantaged."

Something my older brother, Matthew, told me when I started playing football stayed in the back of my mind. He said, "When it comes to making it to the leagues in football, especially the NFL, know that it's a White man's system. And in order for you to even have a chance, you got to be at least two to three times better than the White guy. If you're on the same playing field with them, forget it! They're going to pick the White person. But if you're at least two to three times better, then they *may* consider you."

His advice proved true beyond the playing field, but I was not focused on being better than anyone else. I had nothing to prove to anyone but myself that greatness was in me. And my future capabilities were no longer dictated by other people's assessments of what they believed I could or could not do. The straitjacket of "learning disabilities" was removed, I was ready to escape the institution of the marginalized. I would continually revise my vision until I became the best version of me.

Inner conflict, low self-esteem, doubts, and frustration are compounded by the constant opposition of systemic racism. Feeling invisible, alien, aside from the unwanted negative attention on your skin color – been there. Bucking up on a school system that says, "Too bad. Maybe you should have stayed in the remedial class" – done that. Everyone around you doing the same thing that's leading them nowhere, and living in Hell, but trying to act like the heat ain't bothering you – that was my address. When you find yourself in situations like that, you have to ask yourself some hard questions.

What do you believe about yourself? Has a lie invaded your future – like cancer invades the cells of the body – and convinced you that you have no other option but to let those lies eat away at you until nothing is left but a corpse where your life is supposed to be? There's a point in every man's life where you have to make a decision. A wise man can decide to become a fool, and a fool can make a decision to abandon his foolishness and become wise. It is your decision, not your ability, that lies in question. Your life moves in the direction of your decisions.

I had come to a point in my life where I began to literally see things differently as my conscience became stronger and stronger, and as I allowed it to be influenced by that subtle voice of faith. However, I knew I was in control. I had the ability to go forward or make a full stop. I was becoming unconquerable. Still, I needed the guidance of someone who could show me options I was yet unaware of, someone who has walked in places I desired to be but did not know it yet. I was about to meet such a person, and it was an extraordinary encounter that helped me make sense of everything in my life up to this point.

NINE
THE SECRET TO VICTORY

Don't live to fight. Fight to live.

We call her Big Maxine, but it has nothing to do with her size. Her real name is Velma Maxine, and she is my aunt – Mama's sister. She is also my younger sister Maxine's namesake. So Mama called my sister Little Maxine and my Aunt Velma Big Maxine, and the name just stuck.

My aunt was a godsend for me and helped me through a difficult time. In my last semester at Moraine Valley Community College, things had gotten tough for me. Discipline kept me focused, but the heavy toll of working, studying, school, and bills left almost no room for a social life. It was work, school, pray, fast, read the Word. No movies. No talking to anybody. No, nothing. An old comrade moved back in, Loneliness. But this time it was more than being left out on an elementary school playground or alienated because of my appearance. This was me battling with myself, and nobody was winning.

The dull ache of loneliness weighed on me, and I struggled with a lot of self-defeating thoughts. *Look at you! All your brothers have girlfriends or are married. You don't have anyone, just sitting here in this apartment. You're a nothing, man! A big fat zero!* At times I could not tell whether it was loneliness of a companion or just the fact that I had not obtained that "something more" in life I was after. Whatever it was, I was sinking in the quicksand of discouragement, depression, and defeat.

I was in a war, and my mind was the battleground. Thoughts were fired at me at a million rounds per hour, and in those moments, I believed every one of them. Battle fatigue in the form of self-pity set in, and then I would cry and whine to God. My pity parties always ended the same way – I would get that familiar impression to read the Bible. Sometimes I would ignore it, but eventually after three or four times of sensing the same instruction on the inside, I would pick up my Bible and read. It did not seem to matter what I read; the effect was the same. Like a GPS navigating me away from a mental dead end, each verse would redirect me back onto the road I was supposed to be on until I came to the next detour.

Since I was planning to graduate, I did not renew the lease on my apartment. So, for my last semester, I stayed with Big Maxine and my grandmother. Her home became a haven of sorts, a place where I did not have to be alone all the time. I had the entire basement to myself. There was a small den where I slept and a little area with a chair that I used as a quiet place when I needed to talk to God and read my Bible.

I was still working at Greatland Target in Hodgkins, a forty-five-minute drive from Big Maxine's, which was fine until I had car problems. When I called in one day to tell them that I could not make it, I was given an ultimatum: come in, or don't come back. It was a good thing I was staying with my aunt, because for the next four months, I was out of a job. I desperately needed a break, something to turn around in my situation, and after months of being out of work, the tables turned in my favor in a most unusual way.

I got a call from the location where I had been working, and I was asked if I could come back to work. When I hung up the phone, I was still in disbelief over the turn of events that got me reinstated. It turned out that the man who told me not to come back had gotten fired. Someone had reported him for sexual harassment, and during the course of the investigation, the young lady that filed the complaint brought my name up. She told them how that manager had treated me badly and fired me for nothing. Things started to look up from there.

Staying with Big Maxine turned out to be the catalyst for a life-changing encounter. I would often go to my quiet place to pray and read my Bible. I guess she noticed, because one day she walked up to me and handed me a cassette tape and a Bible. I looked down at the big, blue leather-bound book in my hands and ran my fingers slowly across the silver embossed print, *Morris Cerullo God's Victorious Army Financial Breakthrough Spiritual Warfare Bible*. I had no idea what financial *breakthrough* or *spiritual* warfare were, but I identified with anything that had to do with a fight.

I popped the cassette in and leaned forward as I watched the tape unwind. The action of the reels seemed to mimic what I was experiencing as the words of this commander transferred knowledge from his mind to my own. His voice had a higher-pitch and a bit of a gurgle that made it sound like he needed to clear his throat. But it was as forceful and authoritative as his words.

"The church has done a *wonderful* job in teaching the body of Christ how to become sons of God. But we have failed *miserably* in teaching them how to become *soldiers* of the cross!"

As soon as he mentioned 'soldiers,' he had my full attention. But what he said next sealed the deal for me.

"The call to sonship, brother, is a call to *war*, a call to *fight!*"

I thought, my God! I found a Christian – a *preacher* – that believes in fights!

Ever since I was a kid, I loved anything that had to do with war, probably because I grew up in a community where fighting was the norm. Where I came from, you always fought, and you had to be tough. That engendered my fascination with the military and war movies. And now, this man was talking my kind of language. He talked about God telling him to build an army. *There are Christians out there that can fight? Really?* The novelty of that idea hit me like an adrenalin rush.

I ate up every word. I studied the material day and night, listening to the tape over and over until I could recite most of Dr. Cerullo's sayings word for word. He became my mentor – more than a mentor. He was my drill sergeant, training and equipping me to fight the battles of the mind, which according to him was where the real warfare took place. I began to read scriptures about men of war in the Bible, men like David who took down giants and trained a band of homeless men to become mighty warriors. Up until that point, I did not even know there were stories like that in the Bible.

The teachings of Dr. Cerullo became my field guide and reframed everything I previously thought about fighting. He taught me that God was perfect, He did not make any mistakes, and He created my mind to be perfect. I learned that I could do more than I thought with God on my side. No matter what the hindrance, no matter what the forces, I could persevere.

His mantra became my own:

"Jesus Christ died that I may have 100% victory, 100% of the time, over 100% of the enemy's power!"

Once I realized I could be a warrior and a Christian at the same time, I signed on the dotted line. I wanted to be a warrior Christian!

There's a time in every man's life where he runs out of answers and needs to tap into a reservoir of knowledge that he does not even know he needs – a mentor who is powerful enough to break the cycles of mental stagnation and silence the voice of inadequacy. A mentor is not your friend. He is someone who challenges everything about the way you think and disagrees with your present circumstances until he convinces you that where you are is not where you are supposed to be. That is what Dr. Cerullo did for me.

We are the sum of words, and I was being transformed by the words I was hearing. I was being shaped into a warrior that was armed with weapons that could not be seen: words that could penetrate my every thought and intention. I still had internal battles, but I faced them differently. I still prayed, but my prayers were no longer from a defeated standpoint. They became more strategic. I knew I was praying from the winning side of victory, and I faced my battles head-on.

Prayer became my outlet and my inlet. I could take all of my concerns and dump them on Someone who I knew had enough power to do something about them. God had proven to me that He could take what I thought was a life sentence of learning disabilities and completely turn it around. What He gave me was better than parole. I was exonerated and I was no longer obligated to serve time under that sentence. Prayer empowered me to rise above defeat and the hopelessness that you feel when you can't see any way out of a bad situation.

Now Mama was not the only warrior in the family anymore. I became a prayer warrior too and her partner in prayer. My prayers were not focused solely on myself anymore. I prayed a lot for other people, and together, Mama and I took on some of the toughest battles in our family. We prayed for my brother who was involved in a gang. We prayed for one of my younger sisters who was swiftly headed towards dropping out of school and hanging around thugs, gangs, and drugs.

God had given me my own personal rules of engagement. As long as I trusted Him and allowed Him to be involved with whatever was troubling me, victory was sure. No matter how difficult the circumstance seemed, God worked it out. Before long, each of my thirteen siblings came to believe in this God who not only listened to Mama's prayers, but also listened to mine. Each time a prayer was answered, I gained more confidence to face the next battle. Some of my biggest challenges still lay ahead of me, but a major one was about to end. I was twenty-three and finally about to graduate after four years at a two-year junior college.

The weeks that followed seemed to creep by as I wrapped up my final year and prepared for graduation. I managed to finish my last two years strong. I averaged about a D for the first two years, and the last two were A's and B's. So, I was able to graduate with a cumulative 2.5 GPA. Through faith and perseverance, the giant of academic failure had come crashing down!

Saturday, May 22, 1999, was the big day. Some of my brothers and sisters were there, my grandmother – my mom's mom – was there, Big Maxine, and of course, Mama. As I walked across the stage in my green cap and gown and my kente stole proudly draped around my neck, I thought, *Wow! This thing is really happening!* The joy and relief I felt was indescribable! I was so happy I did not know what to do with myself. I was like the six-year-old me who received that Christmas gift after being convinced that Santa was a coward or a lie. My hope had come to fruition, a dream was being fulfilled, and there was no greater feeling.

It was surreal walking across the stage. I graduated with an Associates in Science degree in Business Management. After the ceremony, I sat on the steps of the school that had been my crucible and reminisced. I thought about all the classes I had struggled through from elementary school through college. I thought about all the nights that I cried. My eyes grew moist as I travelled all the way back in my memories. It was emotional and exciting at the same time. Against all odds – disappointment, failure, hopelessness, pain, and everything else – the impossible had happened. I did not give up when I wanted to give up. I did not take the easy path of failure. I had endured. I had persevered. I walked across the stage and graduated from college! Now I was done. Then it hit me. *What are you going to do after this?*

After a small celebration with my family, we went back to my aunt's house, and as soon as I could, I found a quiet place to be alone. I was grateful to be done with school. But my vision could only get me as far as Greatland Target. I figured I would work there for the rest of my life, or at least until God sent me to the missions field. It was time for another talk with God.

"Lord, You've done so much for me."

I spent some time thanking God for all that had taken place and for helping me to get this far before I continued.

"Okay. I'm ready to go. You want to put me on a mission field. Let's do this thing!"

I was pretty fired up. The prospect of new adventures in some faraway land was exciting. I had enlisted in God's army as a soldier, a warrior, and now I was ready to conquer unknown territories.

"I graduated from college, Lord. I'm ready to go! Put me on the mission field and do whatever! I'm ready! I received training. Now I'm ready to battle for others!"

God's response stunned me into silence.

No. Go back and get your four-year degree.

I had developed a good relationship with God over the years, and He had always been straight to the point with me. But this time, I thought He had to be joking! Yes, I had graduated, but I still did not like school at all. I had hunkered down for four years just to get an associate's degree. I did not want to spend another day in college, so going back was nowhere on my radar.

"What?! Get a bachelor's degree? This is crazy!"

But I knew I heard Him correctly. I had learned His voice by now. I shook my head in disbelief and sighed as I reluctantly resolved in my mind. *Okay, I'll go.*

Trinity was a local Christian college in Palos Heights, Illinois. I thought I might have a better experience among other Christians, so I applied. No response. My sister, Matilda, was at Northern Illinois University. I did not want to go to a secular university, but it was the only door that was open to me. I applied, and that was the start of a whole new adventure.

I had been working at Greatland Target for four years by this time and had received a couple of promotions in the years I was there. Even though pay came with the promotions, it wasn't much. I was training people who were coming straight out of four-year colleges and starting with salaries of $35,000 a year. Meanwhile, I was working fifty hours or more with time and a half, and I was only making $22,000 a year. The forty to forty-five minute drive to work sometimes turned into an hour or an hour and a half depending on traffic. All of a sudden, spending my years at Target wasn't so appealing anymore. I still wasn't thrilled with the idea of going back to school, but if I did, chances were that I would at least have a shot at a better salary.

In my quiet prayer time, I questioned God.

"Why do I have to go back to school for You to bless me with some money?"

His answer did not change.

I was in a quandary. I needed to make more money, but the only way I could make more money was to go to school and get a bachelor's degree. But to go to school, I needed money, and I did not have it. I could not use my parents' income to apply for financial aid, and I was a year shy of applying as an independent. You have to be twenty-six for that. So, I was trying to figure out a way to get financial assistance. In my inquiries, someone recommended Ada S McKinley

Community Services for financial aid assistance. The closest location, however, was located in Dearborn Homes Community Project. I had to go back to the ghetto.

Ada S McKinley was located in Bronzeville, which was a euphemistic moniker for the area that was known as the racially fraught Black Belt, Black Ghetto, or the openly racist, 'Darkie Town.' In its heyday, Bronzeville hosted its own version of the Harlem Renaissance. The community was once home to 2,000 Black businesses, three Black hospitals and six Black newspapers. People flocked to the area during the Great Migration to be part of what was then a thriving, Black metropolis. Residents were squeezed into a narrow strip of land on the South Side between 22nd Street on the North and 51st Street on the South.

Some of the first Black street gangs formed in the Bronzeville area. By the 90's, dope dealers and killers ran the neighborhood, and the Black middle classes moved out. 1999 marked the beginning of early attempts at revitalization, but let's just say it wasn't necessarily a safe place to be at that time.

Typically, whenever I had to go to a location in the inner-city, I would always be thinking about what type of gangs are in the area, what type of activity is going on, what I have to do there, and how long I would have to be there. It was like shifting back into a military mindset when you are about to enter a warzone. Normally, the entrances and hallways of the projects would be lined with guys, most of whom did not live there. Sometimes you couldn't even see the front door, and you would not be able to just walk up and excuse your way through the crowd. They would want to know who you are, and why you were there. But that day, there wasn't a soul in sight, so I just walked right in.

The office was a small, dusty, afterthought of a place. The walls were dirty, and the tiny space was crowded with three old desks and three chairs. There was one guy in the office, kind of heavyset, maybe around 5'6". He looked up when I came in.

"How can I help you?"

"I'm here to try to get some financial aid assistance." I was hoping to be in and out.

"Okay, great. Just have a seat, my man. Do you have your W-2 form?"

I pulled my paperwork out. "Yes, I have it right here."

He glanced at it. "Okay. I'll see what I can do."

He took the paperwork and started typing in some information, switching his attention from the screen to my W-2 and back. He paused a little longer at the screen, then handed my paperwork back to me.

"I can't do anything for you."

That was definitely not the response I was expecting, and it took me a moment to process what he said.

"What? What do you mean?"

He looked me dead in the face. "You make too much money."

I jerked my head back in surprise. Now I was really confused!

"What do you *mean*?"

He lowered his head slightly and raised his eyebrows. "You make too much money. So, what you do? Spend it on rims?"

The smirk on his face made me want to reach across the desk and give him some five-fold ministry. I was hot! *Did this man just insult me?* Even though it was common in my home community to do stuff like that, I felt offended. It was like he was calling me an idiot, at least that's how I took it.

"No, I didn't!" I was noticeably agitated. "I had rent to pay. I have a car note. And ..."

I practically gave him a run down of all the things I paid for each month, which made me even more irritated. He leaned back in his chair, completely unbothered, and waited for me to finish.

"I can't do anything for you."

After that, we exchanged some words back and forth, and I was getting more and more frustrated.

I threw my hands up. "This is ridiculous! Here I am trying to go back to school and get some type of assistance, and you're literally telling me that I made too much money! How is that possible, man? How is that *possible*?"

That seemed to be the straw that broke the camel's back. He assumed a 'let me set you straight' posture and stared at me hard before he spoke.

"You know what?" He paused, almost as if trying to decide if he should say what he was thinking. Then he continued.

"This ain't anything personal, but you know, *I* don't even qualify."

The statement caught me completely off guard, and I could feel the tension easing.

"I've been working here for over seven years, and I only make $7.50 an hour." He leaned back in his chair and let the words settle in the dusty air.

I was stunned! I did not say anything, but my thoughts were loud. *This is crazy the way this system is set up!* Then I heard that familiar quiet voice inside. God was speaking.

Communicate with him. This man is here to help you. Understand his situation. Be humble. He has got to help you.

Now I was ready to answer. "You know, I really appreciate what you're doing here. But the reason I don't have the money to afford going to NIU is because I made the decision to go to Moraine Valley Community College, which is in a Southwest suburb of Chicago. I wanted to do something better with my life."

He folded his arms across his chest, but the gesture seemed to express interest as he keyed in to what I was saying.

I continued. "I wanted to avoid all the distractions that come with the inner-city and the gangs and stuff like that. In order to do that, I had to get me an apartment out there. My parents initially helped me, but I had to get a job and pay my own rent."

And I explained to him exactly how my money was spent. When I was finished, he leaned back in his chair and folded his hands across his waist.

"You know what," his voice was a little quieter than before, "I do have a contact that knows someone at NIU. I'll see what I can do. Just hold on."

He picked up the receiver and started dialing. He held the phone to his ear and then put it back in the cradle. No answer. Then he snatched it back and dialed a different number. I could feel my heart beating faster as the person answered. He started explaining my situation to the man on the other end.

"Is there anyone at NIU that could help?"

Suddenly, he grabbed a pen and poised it over the sticky notepad in front of him. "What's his name? Wha–? Spell it for me." He scratched down a name. "What's his first name?"

He laughed as he wrote the first name, "Well, at least he's got *something* American!"

I looked over at the sticky note. I could make out 'Charles,' but I needed some help with the last name, O-g-u-n-d-i-p-e.

He tore the sticky note from the stack and handed it to me with the gentleman's number on it.

"No guarantees here, man. But if anyone could help you, this is your guy. He's the guy at NIU."

I took the note and thanked him. Mission accomplished, because I wasn't leaving that office without any help. I did not even bother to call. I left the projects and drove the eighty-five miles straight to DeKalb County and went straight to the financial aid office.

Charles Ogundipe was the assistant financial aid director at NIU.

"I'm here to see Mr. Ogundipe, please."

I briefly explained my situation to the lady behind the desk and showed her the handwritten note with Mr. Ogundipe's number. She called him to see if he would meet with me since I had no appointment. I could overhear his heavy Nigerian accent underlaying his crisp British pronunciation.

"Yes, I'll see him."

The lady nodded towards his office.

"You can have a seat over there."

I sat outside his office for about twenty minutes before I finally got to go in. I walked in not knowing what to expect but determined to get what I came for.

"Please have a seat, Mr. Johnson."

Mr. Ogundipe had a short afro and bushy eyebrows that framed the top of his rectangular glasses. And when he smiled – which he did often – I couldn't help but notice the wide gap between his two front teeth. When he spoke, his voice was calm and confident. I immediately felt at ease. He reviewed my paperwork and nodded politely as I explained my situation to him. Within minutes, he identified four different types of student loans that I qualified for and completed all the necessary paperwork right there on the spot.

Your next step may have what seems to be an unnecessary detour. You may even feel as though you are taking a step backwards, returning to the familiar territory from which you want to escape. But every skilled long jumper rocks backwards momentarily before racing forward. It's not a misstep but a measured step that allows you to establish the cadence you need for your next longest jump. Stay in your lane. Maintain your focus. You might not know how everything is going to turn out, but don't stop moving.

I walked out of Mr. Ogundipe's office set up with financial aid and registered to start Northern Illinois University in the Spring of 2000. I could have walked out of that community center with a 'no' ringing in my ears, but I persisted. I did not try to explain the composition of my miracle. Otherwise, I might have talked myself out of it. I had no Plan B; I had to move forward. My persistence paid off and I was officially on my way to getting a four-year degree, and there were more miracles to come.

TEN
TIME AND CHANCE

For every dark night, there's a brighter day.

During my second year at NIU, another moment happened that changed the trajectory of my life. I had started that fall semester with a lot of confidence, and I was beginning to think about how things might shape up in terms of what I would do after college. I managed to finish up my first year at NIU with all A's and B's and a 3.5 GPA, but that did not change how I felt about being in school. It was still a struggle that required me to focus all of my attention on passing my classes. I still did not like school, and I was dreading going to class that particular day.

I had been staying in the dorm since my first year at NIU. That morning, I slung my backpack on and headed downstairs to the common lounge area. As I neared the bottom of the stairs, I noticed a bunch of students crowded around the information desk staring at the monitors above it. CNN was being broadcast live. I walked over to get a better look, but as I got closer, I did not understand what I was seeing.

The lower third of the screen read "BREAKING NEWS." Just then, the camera shot panned from a view of a skyline to a closeup of what looked like a skyscraper. I squinted at the screen trying to figure out what I was looking at as the moderated tone of the news anchor droned on in the background.

"CNN Center right now is just beginning to work on this story, obviously calling our sources and trying to figure out exactly what happened. But clearly something devastating happening this morning there on the south end of the island of Manhattan."

It looked like something had taken a bite out of the side of the building. Thick, dark smoke was tumbling out of the opening and from the back and side of the building.

As the reports continued, I could detect a slight edge and tremor in the voices of the alternating anchors.

"That is, once again, a picture of one of the towers of the World Trade Center."

I still could not wrap my mind around what I was seeing on the screen. I turned to one of the students who was already there when I arrived.

"What's going on?"

His eyes never left the screen. "We're under attack."

And with those words, what started as a typical Tuesday morning became a day I'll never forget.

As I stood there watching intently, I could feel my stomach tightening as I tried to process what I had just heard: *America is under attack*. Then, out of nowhere, the shadowy image of an airplane appeared on the screen and smashed into the second tower. I watched in horror as the building burst into flames and smoke mushroomed up into the air. The only movement now was on the screen. Everyone in the lounge was as motionless as the still frame of a snapshot you wished you had never taken. The tower was not the only thing falling. People were also falling as they started jumping from windows, choosing one desperate inevitable form of death over another.

This was a defining moment in the history of our nation, in the families of the victims whose lives were snatched from them, and those of us who watched the tragedy unfold. Decades would be spent trying to figure out who those people were who were captured on film as they plummeted to their untimely deaths. This holocaust forced many of us on personal journeys of discovering who we were and what was really important. For me, it was my purpose – what I believed God had put me here to be and do.

9/11 had left a cloud of doubt over the certainty of life. We came to grips as a nation with the reality that we are not invulnerable, and that life is a series of meaningful moments on a timeline that can be interrupted in a flash. Sometimes the ground has to shake for you to move, and 9/11 caused mine to rumble beneath me. Playground days were over. It was time to make my life count more than ever before.

My pursuit of God intensified. Every opportunity I got, I spent reading the Bible and talking to God trying to make sense of the rapidly changing landscape of life. Studying the Bible had the same effect on me as it did with my ability to learn in school.

My mind opened up, and I began to understand that even pain could be repurposed, and the most tragic events could lead us into a greater appreciation of others and life itself. The more I read, the more I discovered about God, and the more I understood about Him, the more my life made sense and every question was answered.

I discovered myself in my discovery of Him, and I wanted others to do the same. But I quickly found out that not everybody wants change. My first set of roommates taught me that. It bothered them to see me reading my Bible, and they would get offended when I turned down their invitations to go drinking or partying. All I wanted to do was be a light and help someone to see what I saw, but sometimes I felt like a naked light bulb, shining with no shade.

It takes courage to not fit in. Most people are used to moving around in the dark – the darkness of ignorance, the darkness of fear, the darkness of violence and hopelessness. And when you start to shine, their eyes strain from the brightness, and they begin to see things that confront their previous realities. They may not want what makes you shine. They may not want to be embraced by the kind of transparency that makes your glow possible. But somebody's got to be light, even when that means hanging in solitary places so others can see further.

Being light costs you something. It may cost you some popularity or the comfort of blending in with everybody else. Some relationships may drop off like rocket boosters because they don't have the mental, emotional, or spiritual fuel to go where you're going. But shine anyway.

Don't get me wrong, I wasn't perfect, not by a longshot. On more than one occasion, the hood in me came out, and I was ready to channel every warrior in the Bible I had read about.

And for the most part, I was still pretty much a loner. I wanted connection, but not at the cost of compromise. Eventually, I found a small group of young men on campus who wanted something different from the Greek fraternities. They were starting a Christian fraternity, and I was the first to join. It felt good to finally be around people who were moving in a similar direction as I was. We had small-group Bible studies and were able to organize different types of Christian events. That's how I met Emma.

I had become a young man of consecration. I had not planned to be; it just happened. Consecration meant I was after whatever God was after. However, there was one area of my life that I had not fully committed to God: *women*. When it came to women, I had my own ideas. Naturally, thoughts would come. *You're getting older. You need to go out and find somebody.* But when those thoughts would cross my mind, I would throw it to God because I did not want any distractions.

"Lord, You know all things. You know me better than I know myself. I don't want anything or anyone to hinder Your plan and Your purpose for my life."

I did not want to take the chance of picking the wrong person and messing up my life and future. So, I said, *Lord, You pick her*. I was razor-sharp focused, a soldier in God's army. I was not actively looking for a woman, but let's just say I was noticing some, especially if they reminded me in some way of my mom. Mama embodied everything in a woman that I thought I wanted. But I was about to find out that God will bypass what you think you want for what He knows you need.

Our fraternity would sometimes go out to eat or have other social gatherings with our sister sorority. It was at one of those gatherings that I first saw Emma. I was sitting on the sofa with a few of the founding members, and there were about six or seven young ladies there. While everyone else was talking, I was scanning the room and having a conversation with God. *Lord, why am I here?* God, in His usual manner, shot me a response.

A mate.

That was all He said – short, to the point, no further explanation.

My immediate thought was, *Nah! Can't be!* But while my mind was going in one direction, my eyes were going in another. I started scanning the room, checking out each woman my eyes landed on. I looked at the first one. *Nope.* Second one – *nope.* I checked out each one of them. *Nope. Nope. Nope.* I had exhausted the room except for one young lady who was sitting in a chair directly across from me. It was Emma.

We had never met before, but when I laid my eyes on her, God started talking.

If you marry her, you will have beautiful children together.

I quickly appraised Emma from head to toe and thought, *God, I think you missed it on this one.* She did not look a *thing* like Mama! And I just left it at that. Little did I know, God was playing matchmaker on her side too. I found out much later that she was looking at me and thinking, *I can't see myself marrying him!* As of that moment, unbeknownst to each other, we had both reached a mental stalemate, and as the months passed, I actually forgot what God told me about her. She was just a girl that I would see from time to time around the dorms and say hi to, and nothing more.

Graduation rolled around before I knew it. I was happy to be leaving NIU, but for the first time in the history of my education, I had some regrets about leaving school. I had met some great friends. I would have never thought that a kid from the ruts of the Chicago ghetto would end up with two Ethiopians, a Nigerian, and an Indian as my closest friends. We were a tight-knit bunch too. During that last year, we hung out and had fun together. We laughed and joked with each other. They knew who I was, and they felt very comfortable around me and were not intimidated or offended by my Christian faith. In fact, they respected me for it, even though they never missed an opportunity to joke at my expense.

Leaving school was bittersweet because this time I had lots of fond memories, but I was ready to graduate and get off campus before God decided to add some more years to my studies. It's incredible to think that this once uneducated kid, who could not read or comprehend anything and had no goals or interest in anything academic, was about to graduate with my second degree. How did it happen? My only answer was, it had to be God.

Never count yourself out, because 'impossible' is not in God's vocabulary. I was ready for whatever the next step was, but I did not know at the time that a series of invitations was how I would realize exactly what that next step would be.

The first invitation came from a young lady who graduated the same time as I did. She grew up in the same denomination as I did, and physically speaking, she was more what I was after. Her personality was nothing like Mama's, but this one *looked like* Mama! I had started to wonder if there might be some potential there for us. So when she checked to see if I was coming to her graduation party, I told her I would stop by. After the graduation ceremony, I spent a little time with my parents and then drove my car to the banquet hall where the party was being held.

After I got there, I mingled a bit then sat at one of the tables where she was sitting. *Could this be the one?* Just as I was mulling over the possibility of a potential relationship, someone else crossed my line of vision and interrupted my thoughts momentarily. It was Emma. I had not seen her in a while because she graduated the year before I did. Her hair was different, and I barely recognized her. I had completely forgotten about the conversation I had with God the first time I saw her, and after the graduation party, I never gave her another thought.

The next invitation came months later. A group of us decided to hang out at Dave and Busters, and who should show up? Emma. And somewhere between pinball and Pac-Man, we managed to have our first conversation. It turned out that our lives had moved along complementary paths. She was a youth leader at her church, and I was a youth leader at the local church I was attending. We exchanged numbers, and after a few occasional conversations, Emma invited me to participate in an upcoming youth event that she was coordinating.

When the day came, I loaded up a van with fifteen kids from my youth group and drove about forty miles southwest of Chicago to her church. I pulled up, got out the van, and there she was. Up until that moment, I still saw her as the nice girl from around campus who wore baggy, oversized clothes. But that day, it was like I was seeing her for the first time. Her form-fitting black pants and white shirt showed every curve. Her shoulder-length hair was freshly curled like she had just been to the hairdresser. Everything about her was classy! And to top it all off, her face – I was completely mesmerized by how beautiful she was! *Good God from Zion! She looks good!*

I grinned like a kid looking at his favorite candy, but I was still stuck on my preconceived notions about what the woman I wanted should look like. She did not look like Mama, and she was so beautiful that I figured I probably wouldn't be her type anyway.

After that event, we ended up talking more, but I resolved that we could be just friends, and I was hesitant to take it beyond that. I knew I was a different breed, a soldier in God's army, and although we shared common ministry interests, I was not sure what to make of our connection.

As time went on, I began to question my resolve. I felt this strong connection with her, stronger than I was willing to openly admit. I knew something serious was developing between us, so I decided to test her. I would put it all out there and be totally transparent about who I was, no sugar coating. If she ran away, then it would confirm there was nothing more to it. If she didn't run, well, we would cross that bridge *if* we got to it.

The next time she called me, I had my speech well-rehearsed in my mind. I told her how my life was centered around God, prayer, and work, and I didn't have time for much else. I was working the night shift nine or ten hours, sleeping a couple of hours, then spending time praying for whoever God put on my heart. I wanted her to see that I was not interested in things most guys would be interested in, and I was sure that would run her off, but it didn't. She kept calling.

Every phone call deepened my connection with her and raised my level of concern. I was torn. I enjoyed talking to her, but at the same time, I did not think we were right for each other. My conversations with God were peppered with thoughts about her.

"Lord, I don't want to hurt her. I mean, she's a beautiful person. She's Your child, and I don't want to hurt her. You've got to give me wisdom on how to handle this thing."

Emma and I had been calling each other and talking on the phone every day for about six months at that point. We talked about God, our families, goals, desires, aspirations – everything except our relationship. In my heart of hearts, I knew I loved this girl, but the thought of committing made me uneasy. So, I did what most men do when they are unwilling to commit: I looked for the nearest exit.

I picked up the phone to call her. My mouth felt dry, but I was determined to do what I had set my mind to do. While I waited for her to pick up, I reviewed my mental checklist. *I'm interested in her, but I'm not sure she has the same interest in me. And I know that once I commit to someone, it would be for marriage. I want to be the one to pay for the wedding, and after marriage I want to be the sole provider even if she works. But I'm not at a place financially where I can do that yet. You can't be leading this girl on, man. You can't be sending her mixed signals. This has got to be the right thing to do. Plus, she doesn't look like Mama.*

By the time she answered the phone, I had renewed my resolve that this was the best thing for both of us. We exchanged a few pleasantries, and I got straight to the point.

"I am going to take some time off, like a sabbatical. I think we shouldn't talk."

I hung up the phone somewhat relieved that I had done what I told myself I would do, but there was some consternation over what would happen next. One thing was certain, I was not picking up that phone to call her until I got an answer from God, whatever that answer might be. My plans did not include a relationship. I was a soldier. I wouldn't have time to get married or have a family. My plan was to go out on the mission field and continue praying for others. My only caveat was, if God wanted me to be married, then He would have to pick the woman for me. So, I needed Him to settle this.

I was living in my own apartment again and had fallen into my own after-work routine. When I got off work, I would relax a little, and eat something. After that, I would study the Bible, meditate on what I read, then end up in prayer. The day after I spoke to Emma, I followed my usual pattern, lying on my sofa meditating on the scriptures I had read and spending time with God. As I was lying there praying and meditating, I dozed off with a Morris Cerullo CD playing in the background on repeat. I don't know how long I slept, but when I woke up, I heard God speak just as clear as day.

"Do you remember?"

The question was like a trigger for my memory. Every detail of the conversation I had with Him back in my dorm room came flooding back. *Lord, I don't want to marry or talk to anyone that would interfere with Your plan and purpose for my life. You know me better than I know myself, so You tell me the person. I'm okay with not being married. I'm perfectly fine with that. But if there is someone You think I should marry to fulfill my destiny, You pick her.*

It was as though God was waiting for the replay of the memory to end before He continued.

"Do you remember that time when you told Me that you wanted Me to pick her?"

I responded out loud. "Yes, Lord, I do."

"She is the one that I have chosen for you," He said. "You don't have to marry her; you can choose to marry someone who looks like your mom if you want. But if you're asking Me, she's the one."

Then it dawned on me. *Do you realize what's happening here? God, Himself is picking somebody for you. He knows me better than I know myself. He knows Emma better than you know her. And He knows her better than she knows herself.* I sat bolt upright on the sofa, awestruck that God was literally picking somebody for me. It does not get any better than that. This is the best of the best!

"Yes, Lord. Okay."

And once I said, 'okay,' He started to reveal some things to me about Emma, things that I had not recognized. He told me that she was very precious to Him and that I was to take care of her. He also said that I would be held responsible if I didn't. That scared the living daylights out of me, but I was encouraged because God had given me the answer I needed.

I had grown in my relationship with God over the years and learned to hear His voice, so there was no question in my mind that Emma was the one God had chosen for me. When I last spoke with Emma, neither of us had any idea when I would speak to her again, but I did not waste any time. I ended up calling her back the very next day. She was elated, and so was I.

We never dated before then. We met a couple of times, but for the most part, we just had conversations over the phone. We started by talking once a week, and then twice a week, then every day for six months until that day I cut it off for one day. I felt I would be perfectly okay without a wife, but God knew better. I did not tell her right away that I knew she was the one for me. It took me about another week to think through what I wanted to say and how I wanted to frame the words, then I called her.

"Hey, I don't know when it's going to be, but I'm going to marry you."

I did not know because I did not have the finances, but I knew she was the one for me and I wanted to make sure I planned for it so we could do it right.

I held the phone, waiting. After a slight pause, she responded.

"Okay. Then maybe you ought to talk to my dad."

I smiled on the other end. "I'm perfectly fine with that."

We didn't start dating until after I got her dad's approval to marry her. As time went on, she wanted to know what date I had in mind for us to be married, but I didn't even have enough money for a ring.

I remembered reading a verse in the Bible that said, "Give, and it will be given to you." I was a giver, and I believed God was my Provider. So, I told her to pick a date, and that's when we would get married. She picked November 6, 2004, and we started to plan towards it. I did not have the money, but I knew I was going to get it, I just didn't know how.

Emma's father pastored a small congregation of about fifty people. There was a gentleman in her father's church whose wife owned a jewelry store. His wife passed away, but he wanted to bless Emma and me with some rings for free. He brought two cases of rings for us to pick from. Emma didn't really like any of them, but I knew God was working on our behalf, so I gently encouraged her to pick out a ring. Everything began to come together for the wedding. We didn't have that much money of our own, but money came from everywhere, just what we needed. We did not need any sign that God was with us, but He still made that abundantly clear.

My wedding day was one of the happiest days of my life, not only because I was marrying a beautiful woman who was and is an integral part of my journey, but also because I knew beyond any shadow of a doubt that she was God's perfect choice for me. I made a commitment that I believed only God's grace could help me keep. Therefore, I knew going in that only the faith that brought me this far could keep us on this journey together.

My wedding day was even more special because DD was there. He walked over to me grinning after the ceremony and clapped my hand in a handshake.

"Congratulations, son! You did it, man!"

And then, for the first time, he asked about my wife and how our relationship was before we got married.

"Everything was okay, DD. Everything was okay."

He asked quite a few questions, and I just kept assuring him that everything was okay. The timing was almost comical because our wedding day was almost over, and here he was asking about my relationship for the first time.

I sensed he was trying hard to share some fatherly advice that could possibly help. It was a little awkward because he did not have that close of a relationship with me growing up because he was hardly ever around. When I needed advice, I had most of those conversations with Mama. But I knew deep down who he was and that he cared for me, so I didn't think much of it. He was being a father the only way he knew how. I respected him for it and enjoyed the moment. I wanted him to be reassured and feel like he had done a good job raising me. That conversation was the last I would have with him. He passed away shortly after I got married, within a year and half.

Whatever you look for is what you'll find. If you look for the negative in life, you will always find it. If you look for good, you will always find that too, even in the worst situations. That is what makes It possible to be thankful in every situation, no matter how tragic. That does not mean being thankful *for* everything. There's a difference between being thankful *for* and being thankful *in*.

When there's nothing we can do to change what has been, we can be thankful *in* that situation. Nobody wants to deal with death, but when someone dies, we can be thankful that we were able to share in that life or for the perspective about the value of life that we eventually gain as a result of death. Even lost time can be appreciated. Can you get it back? No. But you can appreciate the movement of time and value of time by switching your focus from how far you have to go to how far you've come.

Life is not defined by a calendar, and sometimes we miss what God wants to do because we put an expiration date on our expectations. But as the saying goes, timing is everything. I believe *divine* timing is everything is more accurate. Because when I look back over my life, I can see how God positioned me and took what otherwise would have been a loss at one point in time and used it for my gain later on.

I lost a lot of time in my life. So-called learning disabilities held me back. Injury and the time it took to heal held me back. Financial difficulties slowed me down. But I've learned that what you may have lost in time, you can gain in timing. If I hadn't failed 5th through 6th grades and took four years to finish junior college, I would not have been on the right timeline to meet Emma. We only had a small window of opportunity to meet at NIU, just one semester before she left. We were both in our late twenties when we met, and the odds of meeting someone our age as undergrads was slim and none. But when your life is governed by purpose, God has a way of making even the time you think is lost line up in your favor. Turning what appears to be endings into beginnings is what He does best.

ELEVEN
THE VIEW FROM THE CLOUDS

I know it seems hard sometimes but remember one thing: through every dark night, there's a bright day after that.

My first time on an airplane was when I went with Big Maxine to my first Morris Cerullo conference in Dallas, Texas. I looked out the window and thought *Wow! God is big!* To this day, I have a fascination with clouds. Looking up at the clouds reminds me of how vast the world is and how big God is. No matter where I am in the world or in life, I can look up and remind myself that God is bigger.

Some people think that clouds are for dreamers, but some dreams are for those who are still sleeping. Dreams that focus primarily on personal wants and gains may not necessarily make a lasting impact. Big dreams are not truly big if they only include yourself. So, dream bigger than dreams that only benefit you, and go beyond that so you can fulfill the dreams of others. Dreaming bigger requires you to be wide awake and ready to take charge of your most valuable asset, your life.

My life has had lots of twists and turns, but one of the things that remains constant is that I have always worked and worked hard. As a kid, I moved from working odd jobs to keep out of trouble to loading trucks on the graveyard shift throughout high school. Throughout junior college and my two and a half years at NIU, I worked at Greatland Target full-time, including nights and weekends. When I started Moraine Valley Community College, I initially studied to be an automotive technician because I knew a lot about cars, but I quickly discovered that was not what I wanted to do. DD encouraged me to stick with it. "You'll get paid a lot of money," he said, but I wanted to own my own business.

A salary is the bribe they pay you to forget your dreams. Still, I had to start somewhere, and I was determined to come out on top. Immediately after graduating from NIU, I started working. I had dealt with racism at Greatland Target, but I would soon find out that was training to get me ready for what I would deal with in corporate America.

My manager was Alan Davis. We called him Al. I was told that I needed to learn the business process first, so they brought me in on third shift since that was the only opening available. With Al showing me the ropes, I quickly learned the processes and became the team lead with eleven guys reporting to me. We were getting a lot of work done as a team, but at the same time, I was looking for ways to bring about change or efficiency gains. I wasn't the type of guy that would come into an operation and manage it. I could, but I would get bored with it. I wanted to get in there where the action was because I was a problem solver. But there was one problem I could not solve. His name was Steve.

Steve held the same position as I did, but he worked on first shift. He had heard a lot about me and how I was progressing, and I was the only one with a degree. I never thought of him as competition. As far as I was concerned, we were all one big team working for the same company, but he did not see it the same way. I think he got a little intimidated at the thought of me possibly coming on first shift and taking his position, and so he tried to sabotage me.

I had only been on the job for three months, and when Al called me into his office, I took one look at his face, and I could tell something was wrong. He reviewed the email that Steve had sent to Al's manager. Basically, Steve had accused me in the email of neglecting my duties and making things difficult for the team on first shift. Fortunately, everything we did as a team was tracked in the system. So, a quick review of the data proved the accusation was all a lie. But the story didn't end there.

My shift was from 10PM to 6AM. Since I was the team lead, I needed to get to work before my team and usually stayed one or two hours later after they all left. Steve also came in early before his shift started at 6AM. Inevitably, our paths crossed. It was a moment where I could have easily confronted him. Instead, when I saw him approaching, knowing that he tried to get me fired, I just laughed to myself and greeted him like nothing ever happened. He seemed a little leery in his response, but I did not say another word and never treated him any differently than before.

Six months later, new management was brought into the company, and God gave me favor. The new manager and I hit it off right away, but nobody saw what was coming next.

He said, "I want Montez on first shift."

Company protocol was that you started on third shift, worked your way up to second, and then maybe, if someone retired, you went to first shift. The protests to the manager's request came back from his upper management fast and furious!

"We don't normally do that," they said.

But he was adamant, "I don't care. I want him on first!"

And just like that, I was promoted to first shift and became a high-level supervisor that managed other leads. That was a position that never existed at the company before. It was created just for me.

It's better to let God fight your battles than to try to take things into your own hands. He can come up with ways to vindicate you that you would never think of. And sometimes, you just need to keep quiet and let your character do the talking. Steve had been with the company for ten years, but he allowed fear to control his actions. I, on the other hand, allowed faith to control mine. I had seen God turn situations around over the years with no help or interference from me. Steve had been with the company for ten years, but after only nine months with the company, with God on my side, I became his boss.

Becoming Steve's boss was yet another opportunity for me to exemplify good character. I did not try to be vindictive and make him suffer, and I did not fire him, though I could have. He had skills, and he knew the operations well. He actually became one of my best employees and an excellent resource to our team.

That was the first of four promotions I would receive at this company. The next three all happened in a similar way: management would approach me and tell me they had created a new position for me. I never sought out or applied for any of them. It was all God's favor. But the fourth promotion gave me a brand-new perspective on how God's favor can work.

A position was posted for an IT Manager in another part of the company. I did not have any intention of applying for it. But after a couple of weeks my manager approached me.

"Hey, Montez. Let me have a word with you."

I got up from my chair and followed him into the hallway. He stopped in front of the bulletin board where the job posting was.

"Look at this," he said motioning to the board. "Why don't you apply for this?"

"Well, I didn't apply because I looked at the qualifications for it, and I don't have five years managing IT projects."

He looked at me and smiled. "Don't worry about that. Could you go ahead and apply? I think you'd be a good fit."

I was shocked, but I figured why not? I had nothing to lose since I hadn't planned to apply for it anyway.

When they interviewed me for the position I was at the hospital because my wife had just given birth to one of our sons. Soon after, I got the call.

"Congratulations, Montez! You got the position."

I was completely shocked because I knew that I did not qualify for that position. Once again, God was working behind the scenes on my behalf.

Looking back, I realize that whenever there was a major event happening in my life – my engagement to Emma, our wedding, the birth of one of my children – I got promoted. That was the pattern. It was as though God anticipated my needs and made provision for them in advance. It got to the point where I was living totally by faith, knowing that whatever I was going through or was about to go through, God was going to show up. God's proven track record became my anchor when trouble hit my life. I vividly remember one such occasion.

I always wanted Emma to have the freedom to not work a nine-to-five if she did not want to. As our family began to grow, it just made sense for her to stay at home with the children, and that was what she wanted to do. Eventually, our family of two became a family of four, me, Emma, and our two children. By that time, we had moved from our apartment in Lisle, Illinois to a three-bedroom townhome, and that was when the trouble started. We had been doing well financially when we closed on the home, but the bills soon started piling up. I trusted God to provide, but my faith was about to face one of its biggest tests, and it started with a dream.

One morning as I prepared to leave for work, I prayed with Emma as I usually did. Then just as I went to go downstairs to leave, I turned around and told her some alarming news: the vice president was going to lay me off. That was the dream. Strangely enough, the dream was not given to me; it was given to Emma. She was even shown the specific date when I was to be laid off. All of it was disturbing, but there was one part that really puzzled me. In the dream, the vice president asked me a question: *"Can you believe God through this?"* And before I could answer the question, Emma woke up. But I would soon find out the answer to that question because that dream was about to become my reality.

After eight years with my company, four promotions, and holding the position of IT Project Manager, I lost my job. The details of the dream proved surprisingly accurate. The date I was to be laid off was almost to the exact date given in the dream. And the person who laid me off was the Vice President and director of the IT department. The dream gave me confidence that since God had shown us what would happen, He would provide for us in the days ahead. But things quickly went from bad to worse.

For the next nine months I was out of work. The severance package I received ran out within three months, and we had only a little left in savings. Six months in, I started a real estate company. I got my LLC, rented a little office, and I was believing God that this was the solution to our problems. I thought I was moving in faith, but maybe it was hope because faith always works, and the business wasn't working.

I started looking for deals, but I could not find any, not one. I just couldn't get the business off the ground, and I was struggling! It got to the point where we got behind on our mortgage and our house went into foreclosure. If it had just been me that would have been bad enough, but I had a wife and two young children. From time to time, I would hear the question from that dream echoing in my mind, *"Can you believe God through this?"*

I was getting unemployment, but the unemployment was only enough for food. I couldn't even afford to put gas in the car. It was one of the most challenging times of my life! Out of desperation, I took a job as a contractor at JP Morgan Chase, and for the next two years, we lived from hand to mouth because the job paid next to nothing. Then right in the midst of all of our financial difficulty, we found out we were expecting another child. So, there I was, no permanent position, insufficient income, and no insurance to cover my wife and our baby on the way.

One night when everyone was asleep, I went downstairs. I was deeply troubled. I was struggling to take care of my family. And to make things worse, I was not in any position to help anybody else, which was my desire to do. I needed to talk to God. I got down on my knees, and it was like a dam broke in my heart. I didn't hold anything back. I talked to him about the layoff and how it was affecting my family, especially Emma. I talked to Him about our home being in foreclosure and not being able to get the real estate business off the ground. I talked to Him about not being able to give to others.

I told Him everything that was troubling me. I reminded Him of promises He had made in the Bible, promises I took as His personal word to me. I mentioned scripture after scripture about His promise to provide and to make me financially self-sufficient. He promised me in His Word that I would prosper, and I felt like I was doing anything but prospering.

This was not the wish list of a little kid who was waiting for Santa to show up on Christmas morning. These were real needs, and I needed God to show up right then and there. After I had poured my heart out to Him, I made one final plea.

"I have done everything You have asked me to do. Now, here I am. I have been obedient. And so, Lord, I'm waiting for You to tell me what I am doing wrong."

Then I kept quiet, and He spoke as clearly as if He had been sitting right next to me.

"It's because of your faith."

I was so happy that I got an answer, I wanted to jump and scream. Instead, I just rolled on the floor so I wouldn't wake everybody. Now that I knew what the problem was, I could attack it. The only way I could deal with this particular problem was to pull out my heavy artillery. I had to use the Word of God.

I thought about how God spoke the things He wanted into being, and I decided to do the same. Instead of complaining about how things were, I started talking about how I wanted things to be. I affirmed God's promises every day, firing them like projectiles at the obstacles in front of me. They had no choice but to come down. And about one week before my unemployment ran out, I finally got some traction with a staffing agency.

I applied for a position as an IT business analyst at a company in Bolingbrook, IL, so I could get a full-time position with insurance. I had the first interview just before my wife went into labor. Then I was called back for a second interview right after my daughter was born. I had the third interview when I went to pick Emma up from the hospital, and after nine months of struggling and another two years of barely making ends meet, I got the job.

God used my position at that company to push me out of my comfort zone so I could grow in ways I never imagined I would grow. For the first time in my life, I was dealing with clients face to face, people who represented global corporations. Once upon a time, I couldn't even spell contract. Now I was negotiating and managing contracts worth hundreds of thousands of dollars. I received three promotions at this company, and once again, they all happened the same way.

Some upper-level management person would approach me and invite me to apply for the position before they even posted it.

There are times when what looks like a problem is a blessing in disguise, and what looks like a detour or roadblock is God rerouting you to follow paths you would not have followed on your own. All of the difficulties I experienced were what God used to favor and position me for my next opportunities. He orchestrated every promotion I received and perfectly timed them so that I would have enough at the exact moment I needed it. He had proven His faithfulness throughout my life, and I was about to discover how He could make even a problem pay you for your trouble.

The director who hired me was asked to move to corporate headquarters, but he did not want to relocate. So, I was then promoted to acting director, managing the entire IT department after only a year and a half with the company. Just as I was settling into my new position, the parent company decided to sell the division I was in to a new owner. I, and everybody else in the division, was about to be out of a job.

In the process of searching for something else, I was approached by headquarters and asked to stay. Mind you, they were still selling the company, but they offered me a $10,000 retention bonus to stay until the company was sold. I was the only person in the company who was asked to stay. Not only that, but they also offered to "make room" for me at the corporate office. That meant another promotion. So, I received the $10,000 and got promoted again right before they sold the company. And the story doesn't end there.

I was promoted to another service division and became the director of IT through another strange turn of events. I was with the company for another six months under the new ownership when the director I was under decided to retire. In fact, the company was forcing him into retirement, and they gave his position to me. There was only one condition: I needed to relocate. The company gave me another $20,000 cash to make repairs to my existing home so I could put it on the market. Then they covered all of my relocation expenses. One of the relocation managers told me that it was unusual for the company to do that.

My family and I stayed in corporate housing for three months for free, and in addition to that, they covered all of my moving expenses – the marketing of my home, the realtor's fees, movers, everything! I did not have to spend one dime to relocate or sell my home. When it was all said and done, when my house sold, I walked away with over $60,000 in profit and all expenses paid.

Adversity is the bread of champions. Hardships are a part of life. But your grit and determined positive response to adverse circumstances and hardship gives birth to the leader in you. Every war has an end, and once you win the war, the battles are easy. But you have to adapt the mentality of a soldier and endure to the end. Whatever it is you are going through, ask yourself the same question that was asked of me: *Can you believe God through this?* Then remember my story.

Developing my relationship with God and learning to recognize His voice was my biggest advantage, even when what He told me to do seemed unreasonable, illogical, or impossible, like the time He told me to go out and buy a bigger house when the one we were living in was in foreclosure. It didn't make sense, but it made faith, and it worked. He may not tell you to do anything as drastic as what He told me, but He will back up whatever it is He tells you to do.

It is possible for a man to go higher than he's ever dreamed. I escaped the thug life, poverty, and prison. I just wanted to make it out of the ghetto alive, but God gave me so much more, and He can do the same for you. So, look up, but don't stop at the clouds. Rise above them, because that is where God-sized dreams are found. You don't have to get there all on your own. You can leverage the access and knowledge that others have provided. Most importantly, God is with you, and faith in what He tells you makes you invincible.

TWELVE
SEE YOU AT THE TOP

Don't leave this world without giving it you.

By the grace of God, I am what I am. I've come a long way from being that lost kid who idolized thug life growing up. I've been blessed to experience things that I never thought possible. Finishing school after years of being tossed aside as unteachable was a miracle in itself. Going on to get multiple degrees and holding top corporate positions is unbelievable! God chose a beautiful wife for me, and true to His word, she gave me beautiful children. I've travelled to different places in the world, and I'm far from those days of struggling as an underpaid employee. Now I am able to live my dream of helping others accomplish their dreams. Giving back is one of the greatest crowning achievements in my life. And who better to start with than my own family.

Michael is the next to the youngest out of the fourteen of us. He came up in a slightly different environment than I grew up in because he had all of us to help guide him after we matured. As a kid, he looked up to my older brothers, because in my community, heroes weren't the people who got college degrees, and there wasn't a dream worth going after unless sports was involved. The heroes were the athletes, and my older brothers were very athletic.

When I was in high school and working, my older brothers were the ones who showed up at my younger brother's elementary school basketball games. And while I was in college, they were the ones attending his high school games. He was a very smart kid, but his goals were not academic. He wanted to play in the NBA and make his older brothers proud, but his dreams took a detour when he did not get a basketball scholarship. He had no interest in going to college, but my brothers encouraged him to go to a junior college and get his feet wet playing in the league.

My experiences had given me a different perspective, and I wanted him to dream bigger. He had academic smarts, good grades, and so much more potential than I saw in myself at his age. So, I tried to convince him to go to a four-year college.

"Mike, why walk on to play basketball at a junior college when you can walk on at a four-year college? What's the difference?"

No matter how I tried to corner him, he just wasn't going for it. He listened, but at the end of it all, his mind was made up.

"Well, could you just take me to junior college?"

So, I took him to Triton College. It was a junior college in a suburban area north of the city. They did not have much going on, but he met the coach there and started playing basketball. But I just could not let him settle for what I knew was less than his best. And it was my goal to make sure that he did better than I did.

I had learned the hard way what it took to succeed, but I knew Mike had potential and what he was capable of. He did not have to go through all the stuff I went through. He did not need to go to junior college. He could go straight to university. Rather than pressure him, I resolved to be there for him and give him everything he needed, but I at least wanted him to catch a glimpse of what was possible.

One day during summer break, I picked him up.

"Come, go with me."

He got in the car, and I drove him eighty-five miles to the NIU campus. When he saw the campus and all the activity, even during summer break, his face lit up. It was light years better than Triton. I connected him to Charles Ogundipe, the same gentlemen that helped me with financial assistance to get into Northern. Right there on the spot, he set Mike up and completed all the necessary paperwork for financial aid just as he had done for me.

Mike graduated in four years at the top of his class with a degree in Business Management. I was privileged to play a part in him accomplishing his dreams. In reality, he helped me in accomplishing mine. My dream was to be in a position to give and help others, but a giver can only know true success when he finds someone to receive what he has to offer. My brother gave me that opportunity.

True success and wealth means being in a position to help others and willing and persistent enough to find others to help, even if they don't ask you for help. One day, you will look back and smile with satisfaction at all the people you were able to help. But that begins by first helping yourself, exposing yourself to words and knowledge that pave the way for you to move in the right direction.

A man's biggest mountain is his ignorance, and deliverance happens when your ignorance is confronted. Mentorship, even through books such as this one, is a step in the right direction in gaining knowledge of the truth. And the truth is, nothing is impossible for them that believe in Jesus Christ and take action on their convictions. There's a saying that goes, "If you want what I got, then do what I did." I've shared a lot of my story on these pages so that you can know that the way things are now is not how they have to be. Change is possible. You can apply the same following principles that helped me to get where I am today. Your future can be rewritten. You hold the pen. I'm just here to give you some ink.

Know Who You Are

A lie usually travels faster than the truth, because a lie requires no real effort. Many people form their own opinions about who you are or what you can or cannot do based on false information. Then, when they are confronted with the truth about you, some choose to believe the truth, and some still choose to believe the false.

Some people will just refuse to believe you can make it to the top until they see you there. Then they will have no other choice but to believe the truth or muster up enough faith to doubt what they see with their own eyes. As the saying goes, real eyes realize real lies. You have real eyes that are opened to the truth, and the truth is, you were born a winner. Therefore, you must not be swayed by the opinions of others or what they think or believe about you.

Your very conception proves you beat inconceivable, staggering odds, literally. Your existence proves your ability to conquer the unconquerable and give possibility to impossibility. Before you were born, you were invisible to every naked eye. You existed only in the mind of God, somewhere beyond the corridor of time itself. You were chosen before time began to be a light in dark places, and your birth on Earth was just the beginning, a visible manifestation of what was hidden before time began.

You made it to where you are today, regardless of what you had to go through. Now it's time to disregard the labels that are put on you to hold you back and start telling yourself something different. God gave you life for a purpose, and to ensure that you were well able to fulfill that purpose, He gave you an ability like no other. That ability is what I call the grace to be number one.

Societal norms, culture, social media, systems, broken people, and life in general will try to tell you that you are not good enough, flawed, and incompetent. But that's a lie. Even if you tried something and failed, that failure is simply a steppingstone to success that has not yet been realized. Your time on this Earth has not yet ended, which means there is more to see if you make a decision to be relevant.

Nothing can hold you down to the ground once you know the truth about who you are, and that transformative process starts with the thoughts you choose to entertain. Look that lie square in the face and tell it the truth and nothing but the truth. The truth is, you are free to rule and reign in every area of your life. The truth is Jesus Christ died that you may have 100% victory,

100% of the time, over 100% of the enemy's power! Accept and live that truth for yourself, and then bring that same knowledge of truth to the captives of ignorance.

You become what you think you are, and you will only go where you allow your mind to go. Therefore, think only the best about yourself. Feast your mind only on those things that will strengthen you for the battles ahead. You were born a winner regardless of what society, teachers, family, and even your own mind tells you. You were born victorious. You were born to endure. You were born to persevere. You were born to beat the odds. You were born with all of the necessary components required to dominate in every area of your life.

Those obstacles in your way are merely the environment required in order for you to showcase your true characteristics. You were not born to get rid of flaws. You were born to realize your perfection. So, when they put a checkmark in the box next to your name under the "just another statistic" column of life, don't let anybody fool you. That checkmark is written in pencil, not ink.

Discipline

Discipline helps you to become the sharpest version of yourself. It is a blade smith that takes the raw materials of your life and shapes and forms it into a useful implement. If you want to be the sharpest in life, be prepared to be placed in positions others are unwilling to be in. Train yourself to be uncomfortable, knowing that part of success in anything is developing resilience by doing difficult things.

Discipline starts with a decision to remain committed. Discipline requires you to stay in position even when you're exposed to the hardest and grittiest circumstances. It forces you to endure critical extremes and tempers you so that you can be strong but flexible enough to bend without breaking.

Every worthwhile opportunity involves a degree of discipline, whether it be getting up every day to go to a job that is barely paying enough, or maintaining your relationship day in and day out. Take advantage of every opportunity to exercise discipline, no matter how small or insignificant that opportunity may seem. You have no time for bitterness. You have no time for anger to take control of you. You have no time to be vengeful. You have no time for lust or greed. You have no time to wallow in disappointment. You have no time for fear. You have no time to entertain regret. You have no time to indulge in self-pity. Nor do you have time for hatred or murder. My friend, you have absolutely no time to waste!

For that reason, you must concentrate on what matters the most, and be tenacious. Do more than is expected of you. Be the first one to come in and the last one to leave. Don't wait for a performance review. Be your own standard. Compete with yourself until you are the best you can be. Make that commitment to exercise discipline. Nothing else matters until your mission is completed. Nothing!

Perseverance

Perseverance without faith is impossible. Faith is part of your genetic makeup. It is the reason you hope. It's a part of what makes you see the invisible and do the impossible. It is what keeps you going despite circumstances. The faith to persevere is based on knowledge – the knowledge that what you see right now is not all there is, and the knowledge that circumstances can be changed. That knowledge is based on the truth, and there is no greater truth than that which comes from God who is Truth.

God's Word is truth that empowers you with sticktoitiveness so that you do not quit when things get tough. His truth keeps you encouraged so that you do not give in to negative emotions. His truth gives you the courage to move forward with dogged determination in the face of fear and failure. His truth keeps you from wallowing in past bad decisions knowing that something better lies ahead. His truth enables you to doubt your doubts.

Perseverance is the crucible for character. It removes every excuse. You might still be learning how to crawl, stand, walk, or run through challenges, but stay with it! Endure to the end! Do not despise or look down upon your small beginnings, because your character is being formed for greater. It's not how you start, but how you finish that matters. So, be persistent and consistent in your endeavors. Be set on the course you must follow. History has already been made for you. All that is left now is for you to persevere and push forward into your future. With God on your side, you will not fail. Look that mountain of opposition square in the face and say, *somebody is going to move, but it ain't gonna be me*!

Gratitude

In a world filled with negativity, you need something to outweigh those unsavory circumstances of life. Otherwise, your perspective will be skewed towards the skeptical, and nothing good will come of that. Therefore, you must be intentional about tipping the scales in favor of gratitude.

Negative thoughts, feelings, and the voices that remind you of the lower places you've been, rather than the high places you're going, are unavoidable because you have an enemy who targets the mind. But just because a bird flies over your head, that does not mean you have to allow it to build a nest there. Shoo those negative thoughts away because their only job is to convince you that you have nothing to be thankful for, when in reality, you have everything to be thankful for.

In every seemingly negative circumstance, look for the good in it. I promise you, it's there. Whether it's the limbs on your body that move, the air you breathe, your eyes that see, the child you gave birth to, the mind you have that still thinks, or that internal will of yours that can determine the very path in life you take, you have much to be thankful for. That I can tell you! So, make a decision to give thanks to God every day of your life, and you will keep moving forward and upward.

Pillars of Life

When I began sharing my story with you, I did not tell you the question I asked the CEO at lunch that day because, too often in life, we want to know the 'what' without taking the time to discover the 'how.' Process is an important part of your journey. It is what makes the payoff after the struggle that much sweeter. But let me fill in the missing gaps as confirmation and additional proof that everybody has a story, and we all start from somewhere.

I was one of five executives who sat at the table that day, but I was the only Black person at the table and the only one without a managerial, VP, or executive title that dared to ask a question. And it was a bold one.

"What do you believe were the top three things that enabled you to be successful in life?"

The CEO smiled in response and looked me straight in the eyes.

"That's a great question, young man."

He looked away briefly as he placed his elbow on the table and leaned his chin on his right hand, deep in thought for a moment. When he finally spoke, he was firm and reflective.

"Number one would be family. I learned a lot from my parents, and I am who I am today because of what I learned from them."

I could not help but think of my own parents and how they had helped shape me and, knowingly and unknowingly, steer me onto the path of discovering the truth about who I am. I nodded and smiled appreciatively as he continued.

"Number two would be discipline. I learned discipline while I attended a military boarding school when I was young. And number three would be faith, because sometimes when you go through difficult situations, you've got to believe and have faith. These things helped to form my character, and character is what enables you to be successful in all you do."

He then went on to share how his own dreams, like mine, had been detoured along the way. But he acknowledged it was those detours and disappointments that taught him that character is more important than a college degree. I was so grateful that I had asked the question. His responses affirmed and encouraged my journey in a way I did not expect, and the parallels were uncanny.

Every man needs pillars that serve as the structure for the life he is building. Those pillars are built from what others call failure, struggle, and disappointment. People who are content to remain where they are in life, don't require the same pillars as those who are striving to be the best they can be. But for those of us who know our lives are meant for something greater, any challenges we face are construction material made of stuff that is proven to withstand the worst storms.

Endure to the End

I have shared four of the pillars that have brought me this far: **knowing who I am, discipline**, **perseverance**, and **gratitude**. Underneath them all is God as my foundation. He helped me to see beyond the mirror of failure. He opened my eyes to the truth and enabled me to see through the eyes of faith. He provided for my every need. He equipped me to operate in a spirit of excellence and saw to it that good came out of everything I did and went through. Without Him, there would be no story to tell. I would have just been another statistic.

God is an army all by Himself. When He is with you, you can defeat any obstacle. This was not just another book you decided to pick up and read. This was a call to duty – a summons – to which you responded. Like a soldier who volunteered to serve in the military because of loyalty and honor, you made a decision to do what only a select few have done. You made a choice for change. And now you have gained knowledge and increased your value so that you can be fully prepared for your next great move.

Everybody can't go where you're going. On your journey to the top, your character will be tested, and your motives will be on trial. That will require you to maintain razor-sharp focus on the road ahead. There may be some lonely days ahead, but no need to worry, because you'll be able to wave from the top at the ones that did not go with you. You will be their encouragement, their beacon of light in their night hours, and their example.

The question is not *if* you can make it to the top but *when*. But to get there, you must exercise wisdom in everything that you do. While others are partying, you are praying. While others are sleeping, you are climbing. While others are doing what everyone else is doing, you are doing what only you were born to do. While others are forfeiting big dreams, you are making the dreams of others come true.

My friend, you're not normal. You are not like others, because what others may do, you will not. And when you make a commitment to make a difference, time will stand at attention if need be, because of the grace of God on your life, and everything you need will be provided.

You are wired for greatness, but the choice is up to you to accept it and take continued action. Forget about past mistakes, seize the current moment in time. Your ability is not in question. You've got what it takes, so use what you've got to your advantage and not to your disadvantage. When fear rears its ugly head, look it dead in the eye and tell it, *not today, not tomorrow, not the next day, or any other day*! Feel free to tell your past it's over, and you're riding your new day all the way into your future, because your time is now!

This world is too big for you to think small. Knowing what you know now, how far do you really want to go? Are you willing to go after something even bigger than your dreams? Let me help you out. With God on your side, absolutely nothing is impossible for you! Be selfless, and then dream big so that you can help those who are in need of the blessings coming to you, and watch God make room for you. While some may believe their problems are too big to handle, you are too big to think that small. I'll ask one final question before I go. *Where are you headed, my friend?* If you're not there yet, keep going, and I'll see you at the top.

NOTES

Introduction

1. Grusin, Dave "Good Times." CBS, 1974

2. Dreams Die Quietly

1. Paraphrased reference to Jeremiah 31:29
2. A reference to Proverbs 13:24 "He who spares his rod hates his son, But he who loves him disciplines him promptly."

ACKNOWLEDGMENTS

I have to first thank my mentor, His Excellency Ambassador Uebert Angel. You are reading this book because of his words during a live social media broadcast, where he urged his listeners to encourage others. His messages, books, and life have definitely upgraded my mindset.

Words cannot express my love and gratitude for my parents. Without them, there would be no me. I know, even in Heaven, they are celebrating me.

To my beautiful wife, Emma. Thank you for all you are to me and our children. I love you, sweetheart.

Thanks to my favorite auntie, Aunt Maxine, who paid for my ticket and allowed me to see the world from a different point of view.

Thanks to all my siblings: my eldest sister Nette, who made one of my childhood dreams come true; my two eldest brothers Arthur and Marvin, who I looked up to; my third elder brother Maurice who opened up his home to me when I had nowhere to go; my elder brother Matthew who coached me throughout high-school; my elder brother Mark who taught me the importance of keeping a secret, and then gave me the opportunity to do so; my elder older brother Marshall who was my best friend when I needed it the most; my elder sister Margaret who treated me like I was her "baby" brother; my younger sister Matilda who was my best friend, and allowed me to make mistakes when I acted like I was her eldest brother and Protector in Chief; and my youngest siblings, Maxine, Melissa, Michael, and Marlon, who gave me the opportunity to be an elder brother who was willing to help. All of you played key pivotal roles in my success. Simply put, I am the product of the environment you formed around me.

Thanks to everyone from the Winners Press publishing team who helped make my dream a reality. Special thanks to Aleathea Dupree, aka The Millionaire Writer, who was absolutely phenomenal throughout the entire book coaching process.

ABOUT THE AUTHOR

Montez Johnson is a consultant, entrepreneur, motivational speaker, and change agent who believes "impossible is nothing."

Driven by his passion for helping to upgrade the lives of others, he shares knowledge and godly wisdom on how to change your world.

He was born and raised in Chicago, Illinois, and lives in the Chicagoland area with his wife and four children.

Find out more about Montez Johnson at montezjohnson.com

www.ingramcontent.com/pod-product-compliance
Lightning Source LLC
Chambersburg PA
CBHW071928290426
44110CB00013B/1516